MANAG
IN SOCIAL WORK

A Set of Papers Based on Study and
Managerial Experience by:

Giles Darvill
Amanda Edwards
Barbara Hearn
Joyce Moseley
Brian Thomson
Bernard Walker
Clare Walker

With help from Lucy Fermo, Clive Miller and Ian Rush

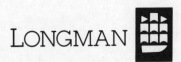
LONGMAN

Published by Longman Industry and Public Service
Management, Longman Group UK Ltd, 6th Floor, Westgate
House, The High, Harlow, Essex CM20 1YR
Telephone Harlow (0279) 442601; Fax Harlow (0279) 444501;
Telex 81491 Padlog

A catalogue record of this book is available from the British Library

ISBN 0-582-09282-5

Printed in Malaysia

Contents

List of contributors

Giles Darvill is an independent trainer and consultant. Giles trains middle and senior managers having been a manager at the Volunteer Centre himself.

Amanda Edwards is a principal social work manager in a hospital setting. Amanda has worked as a manager in London based local authorities.

Barbara Hearn is a management development adviser and author at the National Institute for Social Work. She has been employed in the practice and management in statutory and voluntary sectors.

Joyce Moseley is a Director of Social Services in a London authority. Joyce has extensive experience of community-focused management.

Brian Thomson is an area manager in field social services having managed in both London and Scotland. Brian is co-author of *Developing Community Social Work in Teams* (with Barbara Hearn).

Bernard Walker is an assistant director in a north west local authority. Bernard has published articles on management practice.

Clare Walker is a head of assessment and care for young people in a central London authority. Clare has management experience in field, day care and residential settings.

Acknowledgements

The relationship between editors and authors in the writing of this guide book has been an excellent example of good practice in working together. The work went on uninhibited by different work settings or by the distances involved which ranged from residential to field and Liverpool to London. The critical readers, Rosie Boulton, a first-level manager from Stirling, along with Robert Wilson, an 'about to be' manager moving from probation into a hospital setting gave us the confidence to finalise the work. We thank them, Drew Clode and Alan Dearling for constructive comments. We would also thank Nancy Dunlop, Ann Vandersypen, Nnennaya Onyekwere, our production team at the National Institute for Social Work where the text was developed and co-ordinated. All the other typists who helped each individual author are not, of course, forgotten.

Introduction

During the 1990s, social services managers are likely to specialise in either care management or in service delivery. Increasing numbers will find themselves working for voluntary organisations and some for not-for-profit businesses. A few will become involved in contracting or inspection units.

By the year 2000, social services management may be radically different.. It is likely that polarisation will occur in the make-up of managers — their value positions and aptitudes. Some will wrap themselves in three-piece suits behind barricades of computers, and operate the latest planning and audit methodologies. Others, reaping the benefit of the opportunities of the 1990 NHS and Community Care Act will put themselves at the disposal of different disadvantaged groups and help in the development of services run by, and for, people from ethnic minorities, single women with children, and differently abled people.

The articles included in this publication seek to avoid these polarisations. They were written in the immediate run up to, and beyond, the NHS and Community Care Act 1990 by managers who were struggling to develop a radical approach to community empowerment, but who, at the same time, were keen to understand and apply some of the widely accepted principles and methods of good management in public service, industry and commerce. They were therefore drawing on the two seams which, in a different stove, also fuelled the Griffiths Report on Community Care and the White Paper 'Caring for People'.

We can read here of a number of experiences where an attempt to de-mystify, and share with us, the assessment and service delivery work of welfare bureaucracies was combined with a professional managerial approach to planning, supervision, monitoring and so forth. This is a rich bonus at the end of a decade when the management of social services seemed in danger of developing the polarisations which are feared for the 1990s. Community social work managers have tended to become marginalised from the main stream of social services management. They have been seen as overgrown student radicals with little realism in some management circles. In the era of partnership and collaboration, many more managers have realised that community social work can teach *them* useful lessons. Community social work managers have abandoned a leaning towards existentialism for a new commitment to performance indicators (negotiated with users, of course) and open use of information technology.

Although most of these manager/authors were working in local government, the innovative style and culture of their teams had many similarities with the more radical professionally staffed voluntary organisations. They expressed lessons for contracted-out service delivery.

This publication is aimed primarily at those people who have been appointed recently to a social services management position. In addition, it will be helpful both to those who may be contemplating a career in management and to those managers of some years' experience who wish to reassess and revise their functioning.

One of the problems of reading about management — particularly if you are about to become (or have just become) a manager — is that it is quite possible to acquire an intellectual understanding of many of the relevant issues in isolation from the personal and emotional impact of the role. Obviously, one needs experience of actually doing the job in order to augment the 'theory' of what the job is about.

Nevertheless, in anticipation of gaining a management position, one might obtain a text by Handy, Moss-Kanter, Drucker, Peters and Waterman — or whoever. Such authors can, indeed, make for very interesting and stimulating reading. But, because management is as much about the 'heart' as it is about the 'head', the reader is unlikely to be able to do real justice to the material, having to 'imagine' the situations, the tasks, the conflicts and the dilemmas. Personal experience of the role is either lacking or is too undeveloped to enable any perceptive insights and problem-solving techniques to be related fully, and effectively, to the job in hand.

The source material for this text is the experience of practising managers. Their reflections of what worked — and what did not — help to breathe life into the subject matter. The material itself will assist in the formation of a clear-thinking, objective approach to management. However, management is not all clinical and scientific endeavour; throughout the text it is acknowledged that good management is very much 'the art of the possible', that it involves compromise, and that it cannot ever be a wholly rational process.

The authors would certainly not claim to have all the answers to all of management's problems, but what will be discovered in their writing is a sense of authenticity, of having 'been there'; they have struggled with dilemmas and have developed workable patterns of action, response and resolution. And, for the new manager, to appreciate that others have encountered very similar situations already can be both a reassurance as well as a spur to positive action.

Glossy magazines are not the only publications to have a monopoly on style-consciousness: within these pages the reader will find management style referred to in terms that are straightforward and helpful, and which avoid suggesting that it is either a lightweight irrelevancy or an impenetrable mystery. Practical observations on what style is, and why it is important, will help the reader develop a personal style.

Personal style and organisational culture are connected, and can exert powerful influences on each other. A useful section of the text sets out clearly what 'culture' is, why it is important and how it can be changed.

Some parts of the publication are unashamedly 'personal' in flavour. It is believed that this helps to engender some identification, on the part of the reader, with the subject matter. It also serves to acknowledge the tendency of new managers to be preoccupied with what they are unsure of . . . of what is not going right. The text can assist in turning such uncertainties on their head, and by illustrating them as creative dilemmas which can be resolved positively.

The authors place considerable importance on the need for managers to locate or orientate themselves 'in context'. Analogies with maps are not inappropriate. Sometimes, in order to be clear about directions and destinations, it is necessary to have an overview, to survey the whole territory of your management task, uncluttered by too much detail. At other times, it will be imperative to see that detail — and, here, a larger-scale map is required.

Much of the new manager's experience is characterised by attempts to work out answers to questions along the lines of 'where do I stand on this issue?' or perhaps, 'where *should* I stand, what is expected of me?' The manager may not, for example, have had enough experience of handling authority to be comfortable with it and may be seen alternating between inappropriate over- or under-use in a somewhat artificial, 'forced' manner. No management text can provide the 'right' answer to any problem faced by a manager in real life — not least because any problem or situation is a unique combination of a number of elements (including the manager!) There is, however, real merit in having an understanding of what some of those key elements or variables are, as well as their interrelationship. Returning again to the map analogy, one may be in unfamiliar territory . . . feeling lost . . . but if the current position can be 'plotted', if key considerations are identified, if it is possible to work out possible ways forward, and where they might lead to, then the chances of making a good decision are significantly increased. Note that 'good' and not 'right' are the adjectives used — there is rarely one solution. Whether it's resolving conflict in the team, tackling a member of staff about poor work or deciding whether or not to approve a huge amount of expenditure, the emphasis in this book is very much one of identifying and evaluating contextual factors.

Management can be simultaneously rewarding, demanding, stressful and stimulating; and, contrary perhaps to initial impressions and conventional wisdom, managers do have considerable scope and latitude to decide what should be managed and, how it should be managed.

So, in putting these papers into a sequence, we have attempted to mirror community social work's intention to combine down-to-earthness with reflective analysis and management technology.

Part One provides the very basic guidelines on management, the sort of thing some of us would have given our eye-teeth for when, as managers, we were first required really to examine the authenticity of our responses. When confronted by staff or community groups with a radical programme in relation to race or women's issues. How do you cope with the new loneliness, the looking two or more ways at once when handling your authority? There is an exploration of how a manager might choose a career among the new options presented by recent welfare legislation.

Part Two is more reflective, and explores the concepts which are part of general management literature — the management of risk, change, group culture and so on.

The final part focusses on management control processes — planning and operating budgets, using information technology, and carrying out monitoring and evaluation, concluding with an example of a manager in action where creativity and innovation are brought to bear.

Whether it's managing people, budgets or tensions, the following pages will offer assistance, guidance and, perhaps above all else, a sense that others have been there before — and have survived!

Part 1
Management in
practice

1 Making the transition to manager

'For a short time, I went off my food. People who know me well find this astounding as I have a very healthy appetite and become irritable if I miss a meal.'

'The transition to team leader was hard, painful and lonely.'

The decision to become a manager, which is not necessarily a natural extension of the practitioner's role should be well informed and purposeful. To 'drift' into management would be neither productive nor rewarding.

Some readers may be considering a career in management, others may be already in management posts — by design or perhaps by default. This chapter will identify some key issues in making the transition to management, and will provide a framework for understanding the inherent conflicts, tensions and dilemmas. While this material is drawn from the experience of white managers, it is hoped it will be useful for black managers too.

So you want to be a manager?

Why be a manager? Managers can earn more than practitioners, but there should be other motivating factors. Management is only one option. Today, there are more and more opportunities to develop and to specialise, without going into management. Informed choice is crucial, in relation to what is offered in the current job market and to what you want in your future career.

Assuming you have made the decision to become a manager in the future, it is important that you capitalise on any preparatory learning opportunities that may present themselves.

Can you supervise students, for instance, join working parties or

take any available chances to deputise? Carve out liaison
responsibilities, . . . become a 'lead' person on some issue or project,
and contribute to training sessions. In other words, do some of the
things which will afford you a taste of some of the functions of a
manager. Indeed, it may be possible for you to attend a management
appreciation/potential manager's course which will help clarify your
thinking and perhaps assist in dispelling some preconceived notions
about the nature of management.

Career guidance and planning — in the more formal sense — can
be obtained from organisations specialising in this kind of service, and
can help you widen your experience, aptitudes and skills to suit the
needs of the job market.

We have stressed the importance of making a well-informed,
well-prepared choice of career, not least because it will be manifest in
any job application you make, and in any interview you attend. You
will know where you are going, and it will show!

You have arrived

You got the job? So, what happens now? How are you going to
manage?

All managers undergo a period of adjustment and transition from
the practice role to the management role. It is impossible to say
precisely what form your particular transition will take. This is what
some managers have said about the transition process:

> 'When I became a manager, the only experience I had with management
> was bad and while this was helpful in indicating what not to do, it would
> have been good to have had some indication of the best way to proceed.'

> 'For approximately six months I found the role adjustment pretty
> stressful. I thought about the job outside working hours a lot more than I
> had ever done in the past. I lost sleep. Friends told me I looked pre-
> occupied.'

> 'What I noticed most keenly was the loss of my credibility which I had to
> re-establish at a personal level within the department and in a new role.'

> 'Managers and workers compete — even when you try to make things
> non-combative — and I had been used to a collaborative small team
> approach. But, first-line managers also have to be enablers *and*
> supporters.'

> 'It wasn't that I didn't enjoy the job, but I had a sense of uncertainty and
> lack of achievement, and of putting a lot of energy in without finding
> much stimulation or creativity for myself.'

As these managers discovered, whilst the role will be defined in the
job description, you will need to make a personal appraisal of the role,
and gradually feel your way into it.

One of the things that differentiates one manager from another is approach, interpretation of the role, in other words, *style*. Style is the personalised hallmark of the individual manager: it has its foundations in personal beliefs, value systems, expectations and experience — or sometimes the lack of them!

So style is not entirely a matter of individual choice, but a reconciliation of personal and organisational cultures. It is particularly important for new managers to distil any contradictions between their own and the organisation's expectations of the role, in order for a distinctive, individual style to be developed. This reconciliation is not created one day and adopted the next. It is, rather, an evolutionary process. However, you can start by understanding what you are trying to achieve.

Style is outwardly manifest in the way you do your job, how you conduct yourself in the public domain and what values you project. In a community care context, a team manager's style is likely to be exposed to frequent critical analysis, so you must be comfortable with your style. Make sure it is consistent inside and outside of the organisation.

Some managers' comments:

'I think that style is an extremely important issue because, if we get it right, it allows us to become effective managers who know how to make use of it for ourselves, those we manage and, not least, the service we provide. Unfortunately, while it is relatively easy to articulate the importance of the concept, it is impossible to prescribe. Nevertheless, consciousness and awareness are pre-requisites of change . . .'

'Was I being too assertive, was I being too *laissez-faire*, was I being perceived as being too dominant or too indecisive? I wanted to be myself, but I wasn't sure about that because, becoming a manager, I had become something else.'

'In retrospect, I was able to see that this difficult period was a necessary rite of passage and that the role transition was a significant and substantial one, that there is no change without pain. But in those early days I don't think I was aware of just how much I was thinking about what kind of manager I would be, how I would develop my managerial style.'

Much of the consideration of these issues of style is bound up with notions of power — its use and abuse. Managers have authority and can empower or disempower others. Awareness of your power potential is essential. However you use it, it is likely to have a profound impact on your team, your organisation and on the community you serve. It is useful to think about how you handle your authority. It is, however, inappropriate and unhelpful to reduce style to simple concepts like 'authoritarian' or 'participative'.

Whatever kind of manager you are, or become, there will be

tensions, stresses, and conflicts between your perceptions and expectations of your role and those of the organisation (or perhaps we mean more senior managers?). To avoid these you might, at times, feel the need to act like a chameleon, blending into the culture of your organisation and, 'losing yourself' in the process. There are, however, things that can be done to keep a 'sense of yourself'.

'I read a bit about social work teams, developing staff groups, and went on some good courses. I really started to work with the team to develop the service and took on some new challenges. It is impossible to pinpoint when my transition ended — suffice to say that it did and that through it I made some good friends and started to learn about being a manager.'

'My first move was to get involved — management by walking about. Keeping my door propped open, encouraging the passing person to stop and chat. Breaking barriers needs confidence, but it can be done, even if from a sticky beginning.'

The transition to manager is an uncomfortable time — characterised by loneliness, isolation, vulnerability and confusion — and you may feel overwhelmed and de-skilled.

What helps the manager?

It is very useful to identify supports — both formal and informal — within the organisation. All line managers have been through, or are still experiencing, the process of transition and adjustment, and most will empathise with your struggles, and help you cope with them.

Share your concerns and uncertainties in an open, honest way. It should help you make sense of the process and help cultivate a similar relationship between you and the staff you manage. This transition to manager takes time. It is important not to rush things, or push yourself too hard.

You will come to see teams and colleagues in a fresh light. However involved you are with the team you manage, you are in an hierarchical position in relation to the staff. This difference must be acknowledged. It is part of the transition process which many competent and reliable practitioners find painful.

'There was one issue that I kept turning over in my mind although not always consciously — that was the leader/colleague dichotomy. Certainly, I was a colleague to the members of the team, but I was also their leader. How did I reconcile those, at times, apparently mutually exclusive roles?'

'My team acknowledged that being the manager was not, or at least not necessarily, to be equated with being more knowledgeable, more experienced, more expert or in any way better.'

'It seems to me that, while this might be easy to say, the full impact of being a manager can only be realised when there is an explicit awareness that while managers and practitioners have different roles, their hierarchical relationship is secondary to their supportive one.'

Colleagues now include other managers, both within and outside your immediate working environment. Although you may not work regularly with them as a team, the development and maintenance of supportive links with those colleagues is crucial. In making such connections with these peers, often it will be helpful to become involved in divisional and departmental forums and to volunteer for special project groups or working parties. While the forging of the supportive network might not be the primary purpose of such staff groupings, there is no doubt that it can be a byproduct. The sharing, both formally and informally, of common issues and experiences will also make a significant contribution to your growing appreciation of 'management' in the wider organisational context.

Having a personal project, study, or association with an outside body can also help. It can be your special area and its cultivation can help to counteract some of the demands and pressures of your organisation. It may also help conceptualise and reframe some of what is occurring in your work setting.

Also, and this is very important, take care of yourself. Be in tune with your needs, and treat yourself from time to time. For example, carve out the space in your diary to have a long weekend. To make this happen requires the same forethought and planning needed to attend an important meeting or participate in a training session.

References

Stuart, R. (1963). *The Reality of Management*, pp. 110–25, Pan Books.
Marshall, J. (1986). *Women Managers: Travellers in a Man's World* pp. 159–66, J. Wiley & Son.
Adair, J. (1983). *Effective Leadership*, Gower.
Handy, C. (1976). *Understanding Organisations*, Penguin Business Library.

2 Making decisions effectively

In the course of our lives, we make decisions all the time — tea or coffee? What to eat? Where to travel? And these are personal choices usually based on all the necessary information available. At work, however, decision-making is very different because it is undertaken in response to others including people in our organisation and in the local community.

This chapter begins with some technical or academic approaches to decision-making, and examples of putting these into practice in a community social work setting. These are followed by a discussion of group/team decision-making and its application to community social work. Finally, there is an outline of negotiating, which is important to team managers and to others working in partnership with communities and local groups.

Decision-making

Readers may be thinking that they never have time to think. But, the first stage of good decision-making is clear thinking about what the problem is. Simon (1971) calls this 'intelligence activity'. The second stage is to analyse the nature of the problem, that is to develop or invent the possible causes of action — 'design activity'. The degree to which these two stages are carried out adequately will influence the final outcome — 'choice activity' — the selection of a particular course of action from the possibilities generated.

At the point of decision, it is as well to reflect and be sure of the risk attached to each course of action. Quick decisions are often vital, and it may not be possible to gather all the facts, but it is in everyone's interest if the decision-maker can slow the pace to consider in full all possible outcomes. It is particularly important when the decision is one that will have far-reaching effects on the person(s) involved.

> If an elderly person is seen to be at risk living in the community, unless the risk is a matter of life and death, then the decision to move that person is better taken when everyone involved has been contacted and all alternatives pursued. Network meetings and case conferences are useful methods of doing this. The involvement of local community volunteers and neighbours helps get the full picture.

Managers have to recognise the limitations of their decision-making, and identify the factors which affect their freedom. These limitations can come from the culture of the organisation, economic realities, policy and practice guidelines (see Fig. 2.1).

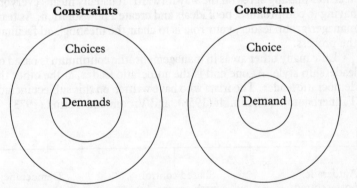

Fig. 2.1 Differences in demands, constraints and choices in two jobs

Demands include: minimum criteria of performance procedures that cannot be ignored.

Constraints include: resource limitations, physical location attitudes and expectations of others.

Choices include: how the work is done, what work is done.

Decision-making, although it can be analysed in three stages, is not an entirely rational activity within human organisations. Lindholm describes the activity as the 'science of muddling through' in an article of the same title (Stewart, 1983). Effective management aims to balance the rational with the non-rational. This means getting

the best possible solution rather than striving for perfection.
Searching for a decision stops once a pattern is found which is
reasonably good and acceptable.

> A team member wishes to spend £350 from the Section 17
> vote, to send a family on holiday. The casework grounds are
> strong, and the team manager is approached to sanction the
> money. The procedure manual says that holidays cannot be
> funded in this way. Before deciding to sign this form, the
> policy and procedure must be fully considered. An
> alternative form of funding may have to be sought or the team
> manager should pass the problem to senior managers for a
> decision.

The process of group decision-making goes through similar
stages. The concepts of consultation and negotiation are to the fore
and also of 'gaining a decision' which is really to gain consensus on a
way forward. Consensus is a process whereby those involved in the
decision-making agree on the way forward. It usually means everyone
having to compromise, pool ideals and create a new solution. As team
manager/group leader, your role is to chair the meeting and facilitate
the process.

Like many other areas in management, the continuum is based on
leadership style. At one end is the autocratic leader, at the other the
democratic leader. Theorists who have written on this subject include
Tannerbaum and Schmidt (1958), and Vroom and Yetton (1973).

Autocratic:	Shared control:	Democratic:
boss-centred	with groups	the group is
leader is in	being consulted	in control and
control and	and sharing in	the leader
makes the	the process but	delegates
decision.	the leader	decision-
	having overall	making to
Fig. 2.2	control.	the group.

The chart (Fig. 2.2) is a tool to help managers locate themselves
and consider how they should behave in different situations and at
different times.

If a team is cohesive and working well then, for example, cases are
likely to be allocated with little involvement by the team manager.

The manager will operate on the right of the continuum. But if it is a new team, or a team new to you, or in a period of flux or change, then, in order to carry out management tasks, you may need to be on the extreme left of the continuum to begin with.

Decision-making with local people

Community social work practice may include involving local people in decisions. If you wish really to engage the members of a group, you need to convince them that their participation will bear fruit. If the group members feel that their opinions are important, and really will be considered, then those people are likely to be committed to helping you find an outcome.

Whilst this is a fundamental tenet in community social work, there are nevertheless (numerous) incidents of this process going very wrong, when consultation with local people proves to be just for public relations reasons and not in order to share in decision-making.

In one instance, the problem was confusion about aims and poor communication. Social workers were told that money had been allocated for a community centre in their neighbourhood. The task set was to liaise with the local community about the resource and its design. A consultation meeting was called, but the purpose of the meeting had not been made explicit. Local people arrived wanting to press for a zebra crossing outside the local primary school. Few people were interested in the community centre design as it was not high on the neighbourhood priority list. The meeting ended with the local community members feeling disgruntled as they had not got what they wanted. The workers did not get the information they needed either.

When consulting with staff and local communities, are you clear about the extent of their involvement? Who will make the final decision? What will the feedback mechanism be to inform them of outcomes?

Involving people in decision-making is a skill, in which team managers/group leaders need to be trained. Training should aim to offer the opportunity to learn and obtain direct feedback on style and abilities, and there are also technical skills which can be learned, including those described below.

Timing First when you convene a meeting, ensure that you have set aside enough time to do the task. Time needed is always difficult to judge but you do need to have space between each appointment, to include preparation time, meeting time and debriefing time. Timing of the meeting is critically important when trying to involve the local community. Do check out what is likely to be the best time to hold the meeting. For example, 3.30 pm is likely to be a difficult time for carers who have small children and 7.30 pm on a winter's evening is probably not a good idea for a meeting with a tenants' group which comprises predominantly elderly people.

The venue Ideally, the venue should be warm, with refreshment-making facilities, and it should be the right size for the group. If people are to be consulted about their locality, the venue should be central to the locality. Is there access for disabled people, including suitable toilets? Have you signposted people through the building, if it is complex?

On the day Arrive in good time, ensure you have all the pens, paper, flipcharts and notes you need.

The chair person is responsible for collating an agenda. If this is a negotiated, participative meeting, those who are invited should be asked to submit items for the agenda before the meeting. It is a good idea to write the agenda on a large sheet of paper and, at the beginning of the meeting, check that the agenda reflects the outcomes you hope to achieve.

It is a good idea to get everyone to introduce themselves. If the meeting is too large, ensure that those convening the meeting are introduced by name, and by any other description that is appropriate.

Note-taking is important in order to provide a record of the proceedings. It is better to get a person other than the chair to take notes on the meeting. If it is a large meeting, it is best for the key points to be written on a large wallchart. In this way, you can note decisions made as the meeting goes along to stop confusion about what has already been agreed. After the meeting, the note-taker should ensure that the notes are available for circulation as soon as possible.

The technical details are easy to follow if, before the meeting, you make a checklist of the tasks, needs, and who is to do what, and when.

Negotiation

It is impossible to give guidance about the process and dynamics of each meeting you may chair, but it is possible to describe some of the processes involved in negotiation.

Negotiation is when two or more parties try to come to an agreement over the way forward. Many engaged in community social work will enter negotiations with local communities over the provision of services and resource allocation. Also, teams have to negotiate for resources and services within their own organisation.

At the outset, ensure you have all the current information you will need. Remember to consider what information the other parties are likely to bring to the meeting. If you have gaps in your knowledge or information, find out how to resolve the problem. Who has the information? Contact them and acquire what you need.

Negotiation is only effective where the ground rules are clear and established. Be clear at the beginning about the outcomes you want. What are the other parties wanting? What are the trade-offs that can be made? Make sure you agree on the limits of the scope of negotiation. If there are issues of content or scope which are unclear, question them.

Often, negotiations get into circular arguments. The task is then to break the circle, which demands creative thinking and behaviour. It is important at this point to remain constructive, open-minded, co-operative, positive and encouraging. If the situation gets volatile, try to maintain a controlled and disciplined style of presentation.

Before agreeing at the end of the negotiation, make sure ends are securely tied! People have different needs and wants, which often lead to different perceptions of what has occurred, unless care is taken. It is important that global offers are amplified with clear details of what exactly has been accepted.

Conclusions

Decision-making is an activity which takes up much of a manager's time. It is important that, if people are to be empowered, more involvement of the community in decision-making will have to take place, as has been advocated in both the Wagner and Griffiths Reports. Skills in decision-making and negotiating are needed by workers in order to enhance their confidence and enable good practice. Although the processes are not complicated, they are easy to overlook, and I believe they are often neglected in training schedules.

References
Simon, H.A. (1971). *Organisational Theory — Selected Reading* Pugh, D.S. ed. Penguin.

Stewart, R. (1983). *Choices for the Manager*. McGraw and Hall.

Lindholm Public Administration Review (1959). vol. 19 no. 2.

Tannerbaum and Schmidt (1958). How to choose a leadership partner *Harvard Business Review*, March–April.

Vroom, V.A. and Yetton, P. (1973). *Leadership and Decision-making* University of Pittsburg, PA.

Further reading
Doyle, M. and Strauss, D. (1977). *How to Make Meetings Work: Interactional Method*. Jove Books. Adair, J. (1983). *Effective Leadership* Gower.

3 Resource management

One of the key tasks for any manager, and one of the most important determinants of success is to manage resources. If you are new in management, this responsibility is likely to be much more significant for you than previously. In the past, you will probably have had some control over spending your time, and delivering your own skill. Now your responsibility will include all staff — their skills and time together — also the buildings they occupy and possibly the resources of local people and groups with whom you work.

People

The most significant resource in the personal social services is the staff. Managers need to pay attention to the personal and professional needs of all staff. The mechanism for this is personal supervision which should not be restricted to 'professional' staff, although its frequency is likely to vary according to role. To have individual discussions with all staff recognises their worth as individuals, their own potential for development, and the contribution they make to the work of the team.

Personal supervision is an important opportunity which should be used to discuss far more than the details of the cases for which the member of staff is responsible. This discussion has to be undertaken systematically and is something all staff have a right to expect from their manager. It does not always happen. A common theme of child abuse inquiries has been the poor quality of supervision of the front-line workers.

Supervision should also consider the personal needs of staff, which should not be confused with 'therapeutic supervision', which projects all the issues on to the personal difficulties of the worker (for example, his or her inability to accept authority). Rather, we are talking about the need to talk formally about career development issues, including training needs and the preparation of an annual training plan.

It is important for all staff to have opportunity for training, and one way to achieve this is to agree that a certain proportion of time must be set aside (ie days per year). Time should be available for all staff, not just for those who request it, or who are good at getting on courses. Once the framework is agreed, then the details need to be finalised as part of the supervisory process. This can be difficult for managers as the staff who are the least keen on training, and resistant to it, are often those with whom you have to be directive, identifying the reasons why training in a particular area is important and what it should achieve. Managers need to avoid colluding with staff who are resistant to training: it is easy to rationalise that they would not benefit from it, and should not have access to it.

It is often assumed, mistakenly, that people are able to make decisions about their future by themselves or that to ask for advice is to appear over-ambitious. In fact, very often, people make decisions about jobs without advice, which they later regret. Advice can be useful about the type and variety of experience that is needed, the dangers of specialising too narrowly, and the optimum time to spend in any one position. Failing to recognise the relevance of these areas is possibly the legacy of the period when 'careerism' was frowned on by many staff, and when there was widespread hostility to management, perhaps the result of the poor standards they found, or because they saw social work as rejecting 'management values'.

If the staff are a manager's most important resource, then their skills are the tools available to do the job, and need to be identified. These skills should then be compared with those necessary for the successful achievement of the team's aims and objectives, which should be explicit and widely known, perhaps in the form of a published statement (see *Creating an informative environment*). The skills of any balanced team complement each other, and there is also much truth in the hackneyed cliché 'that a team is like a chain — only as good as its weakest link'. Developing the potential of the weakest members of a team is often more vital than concentrating on achievers, who are better able to look after themselves.

Good managers recognise that all staff, including those in administrative and manual positions, have the same need as 'professional' staff to develop their skills and gain satisfaction from their work. In a residential establishment, the cook contributes as much to the satisfaction of the people who live there as any of the care staff. Similarly, the most skilled social work will be of less value if the

standard of typing is not good enough to gain the respect of other
agencies, such as the High Court. This is your concern. Always
remember to blame the headmaster, not the caretaker, for a dirty
school.

Newly appointed managers will inherit staff they had no part in
selecting, and with whom they may not be entirely happy. This
feeling may well be mutual, particularly if any existing team members
were unsuccessful in applying for your management post. A manager
needs from the outset to establish the authority necessary to do the job
effectively, yet must avoid appearing dictatorial or 'macho'. Those
with the responsibility for your appointment were confident enough
in you to give you the job. You must have the confidence to do it.

Your first moves are vital, as everyone will be watching you,
recognising your potential for affecting their lives. You need to lay
down the ground rules by demonstrating style and indicating your
plans for the immediate future. It is probably unwise to introduce
major changes too quickly, as it may be more difficult to carry staff
with you. This introductory period should not be allowed to continue
too long, so a target is helpful by which time you will have decided
what needs to be done in the longer term, and have set a timetable to
achieve these goals.

Share this assessment, with the staff, taking care to emphasise the
good things you have found, and aim to build upon; do not
concentrate on the negative things. From the outset, the pattern and
form of team meetings needs to be established. They must be regular
and agreed as the first priority for all staff. Membership should be
open to everyone, but there needs to be an acknowledgement that
some issues may only be relevant for particular groups of staff. The
remainder can be excluded from such meetings as long as they know
why, and are aware of the subjects being discussed and what is the
outcome.

Any team should be more than merely a group of individuals. The
fact that, as a unit, they are 'greater than the sum of the parts' needs to
be recognised. The value of team-building is discussed elsewhere, but
the results of this process need to be recognised as an important
resource.

Holding team meetings is one way of establishing the culture of
the team — by making values explicit. Meetings should also be the
forum where staff have the opportunity to challenge what is
happening in the team. It is important for managers to try to make
sure everyone feels comfortable about being open about values, and to
enable this to take place. There needs to be a mechanism for managers
to check that their perception of what goes on in such gatherings is
shared by others who attend. It is not unknown for the most articulate
and persuasive advocates of openness to actually work in a completely

different way.

It would be naive to suggest that such an approach will stop gossip and rumour. There has never been a workplace where this did not happen. An open management style can, however, go a long way to minimising the negative effects which can be so damaging. For example, it may mean that some of the talk is of how good the work situation is compared with previous experiences, or in spite of frustrating external difficulties!

Managers must also accept that a lot of the discussion will be about them and their performance. You need to be aware of the temptation to become too much a part of the team. Often managers do this as a defence against what they see as a hostile world outside. This was a significant element in the development of community social work but there are drawbacks to this, not least the potential implications for the manager's role in the wider organisation.

Skills

As a critical resource of any manager is the skills of the staff, care has to be taken in allocating skills appropriately. A danger is to match the needs of the moment with the skills immediately available, which, in addition to increasing the dangers of burnout, restricts the development of other staff by denying them the opportunity to broaden their experience. Managers need to formulate a clear strategy for matching skills to demands, which also allows for the personal development of the staff concerned.

The consequence of this strategy is that managers will need to allocate cases/responsibilities to staff who, they feel, will not do as good a job as some of their colleagues. These are difficult judgements to make, as the result is a less good service to consumers than the best available, which can reflect badly on the department in terms of credibility with other agencies. Managers can, however, ensure that there are minimum standards which are acknowledged by all, and that it is unacceptable to fall below them. It is only by broadening experience, and by enabling staff to improve their performance, that the overall level of skills available within the workplace will be increased.

Burnout

One of the most important responsibilities of managers is to ensure that they get the best out of staff. This is particularly important in many aspects of social work, where the personal strains on staff can be great. Managers need to be aware of the danger signs and to take steps to deal with it. Burnout is now acknowledged as a real problem for people who have prolonged exposure to difficult interpersonal situations. It is important for managers not only to recognise this but to help the individual concerned, for example by altering work patterns. There may also be a need to discuss such alterations, and the reasons for them with middle or senior managers, as the underlying cause of stress may be inadequate resources or unrealistic demands. In addition, managers must accept that they too are susceptible to burnout and should take the necessary steps to avoid it. It is crucial that burnout is seen as a natural consequence of the working situation rather than as a sign of personal weakness.

One way of preventing burnout and of reducing stress is to ensure that staff have the optimum amount of variety in their work. There is nothing worse than constantly doing the same thing, especially if it is personally demanding. For example, a social worker cannot be expected to visit families whose children are on the child protection register and do nothing else. Providing variety should not be a euphemism for increasing workload. The proper time and space must be allowed for this adapting to new kinds of work, otherwise job enlargement will have the opposite effect of increasing pressure.

Helping to reduce the chances of burnout through supervision is part of an honest and open approach. Such an approach involves praising good work as well as being critical of poor work. Praise is surprisingly rare.

One classic example of this was a senior manager who was asked to write commenting to a member of staff on some good work with a very difficult case involving some personal danger. He refused to write, on the basis that 'this was what that person was paid to do'. That same manager was the first to be critical when things went wrong. It was not surprising that he was neither well liked nor respected. In retrospect, we learn a lot from bad managers; indeed, they could be said to be the inspiration for this book.

Staff selection

Another key aspect of managing people as resources is the selection of staff. This is an area where managers should have a good opportunity to influence the direction of their services. As with other management tasks, it is not something which comes naturally, but fortunately something many departments now take much more seriously, particularly when it is part of an equal opportunities policy. There are usually personnel staff available who can give much helpful advice and who often have specific training in this field.

No matter which system is used, unsatisfactory appointments will always be made. There are safeguards. Many of these will be covered during the basic personnel training which ought to be offered to any newly appointed manger. To be realistic, however, this training may not always be available if you are only responsible for a small number of staff, and only make appointments infrequently.

A few simple rules may help.

- Have a clear idea beforehand of what the requirements are — and a person job specification. This should include a list of the skills, experience and qualifications which anybody must have to do the job.
- Prepare an eye-catching advertisement which accurately summarises the job and makes it look attractive. Give a contact person with a forename rather than with a title. This will say a lot about the style of the team. Provide an information pack. Putting an interview date in the advert will suggest good planning.
- Give the opportunity for applicants to visit the team, and for team members to meet them. This gives the chance for people to decide if they want to work with you, and also for team members to contribute to the process. (The influence they will have needs to be agreed and defined beforehand.)
- Plan how to find out if applicants are suitable. There is a limit to the information that can be gained in a ten-minute interview, which needs careful planning when involving all members of the selection panel.
- Do not be afraid to ask questions which may be uncomfortable for the candidate, but remember they must be strictly relevant to the job, and must not contravene equal opportunities legislation.

If in doubt, do not appoint — it's always better to take a second look. Do not be over-anxious to overcome short-term staffing difficulties with inappropriate appointments. It's easy to give someone a job, but much harder to take it away. Provide the opportunity for unsuccessful candidates to have feedback on the reasons why they did not get the job — an important process, but not as difficult as it may seem, and often a very helpful part of staff development.

It is also necessary for managers to have a good working knowledge of the disciplinary procedures, which are not a recipe for an authoritarian style of management, but helpful in a variety of situations. If they are to be used effectively, managers need a good understanding of them. It must be remembered that the purpose of discipline is *not* to punish staff but to improve performance. The best

way to use these procedures should form part of the basic personnel
training.

Time

One of the most significant resources for which managers are
responsible is the working hours of their staff. It is a salutary lesson for
any manager to add up the labour costs involved (in monetary terms).
This exercise will demonstrate how vital it is that time is used
constructively and not wasted. Managers need continually to review
how they use their own time and that of their staff.

Managers will need to gain control of how they spend their own
time. There will be a number of activities that will be beyond their
control, such as meetings with outside agencies when they represent
the department, and similarly those called by more senior staff either
in the department or in the authority. Managers need to comply with
all such demands. Indeed, it is important to decide how much time is
to be spent in the company of the team, which should be explicit and
agreed with staff so that they understand your framework for time
management.

Once this framework has been established, including the time that
can be spent away from the work location, managers have a basis to
negotiate external demands which exceed this. It is also important for
managers (and their colleagues) to recognise that they have the same
needs in respect of time management as does everyone else.

Any framework for time management for all team members
should include elements which are sacrosanct and cannot be altered.
Such activities will include team meetings, supervision, attendance at
reviews, etc. Obviously, the dynamic nature of much social work
activity will mean that there are occasions when exceptions have to be
made. These, however, should be few and far between. If they are too
frequent, a number of pertinent questions arise for the manager: the
adequacy of resources, social work practice (including managing
social work emergencies), and avoidance of team participation.

These elements are part of the regular day-to-day activity of social
work practice, but effective allocation of time demands a broader
prospective. A mechanism is required for reviewing the team's work
as a totality and planning for the future, such as team away-days on a
regular basis with a clearly agreed agenda. These activities have a
management function in terms of assessing, clarifying and changing
aims and objectives, and also provide the time and space for creative
and innovative practices to be considered. It is often helpful to have an
outside facilitator for such occasions in order to tease out the relevant
issues from a detached viewpoint. A facilitator's role must be defined

carefully and agreed beforehand.

Such days sometimes are considered a luxury which hard-pressed teams claim they cannot afford, while senior managers may regard them as unnecessary, or as a threat. The benefits of such days need to be recognised by staff, as they will resent the unproductive use of time when there are so many other pressing demands on them.

The supervisory process should include an examination of how people are using their time. The reasons for this must be made clear within the culture of the team otherwise there is a danger that it will be seen as a management mechanism for control. The primary objective is to ensure that staff are not overburdened with excessive demands. It is a mistake to think that people can work at maximum capacity every minute they are at work. Agreement is required about the work to be done and the work to be postponed. Management support in such instances is crucial, and first-line managers must make middle and senior managers aware of the position. Obvious examples of overload include children on the child protection register not being visited or other statutory requirements not being fulfilled.

As part of their analysis, managers need to assess the reasons for an excessive workload, or for any increase in it. For example, more referrals from the housing department may be the result of a change in housing policy, or an increase in the numbers of children in care may indicate a breakdown in the decision-making process. There may be alternative approaches to practice which would alleviate some of the demands on time, such as the introduction of groupwork, the involvement of other agencies to avoid duplication (such as health visitors having direct access to family centre places rather than always going through social workers) or the mobilisation of local people or groups in the provision of services.

Social work practice should not be regarded as restricted to home visits or to office interviews but should be seen much more as an enabling and creative activity. For example, it is helpful to encourage (or demand) that all staff have responsibility for developing an aspect of their service, in addition to their 'normal' work with cases. For example, in a social work team, each member can be responsible for a client group, such as children under eight, or elderly people. This role would involve active liaison with others working in this area, linking with community groups to develop an inventory of resources, and matching this with the perceived needs of the area. For example, someone with responsibility for children under five might work with health visitors, develop playgroups, mother and toddler groups, or health care groups for mothers. Activities such as this can legitimately be categorised as preventative work but are also a stimulating and enjoyable break from other more 'stressful' duties.

The manager's role is to assist in the identification and definition

of the task and to ensure that it is accepted as a legitimate part of the
working week, rather than as something to be done in addition to the
more traditional work, or only when time permits. Managers also
need to recognise that enabling work is a good way of creating
resources. For example, contact with a local vicar whose church hall
was used for a playgroup led to the realisation that the large building
was underused for long periods of the week. After careful negotiation,
it was opened as a day centre for elderly people; a much-needed
resource which the authority's capital resources would never have
been able to provide. Such an approach is not easy to sustain;
particularly as this work is often the first to come under pressure to go
during times of high demand or staff shortage. Just as is the case with
team days, this must be accepted as a necessity rather that as a luxury.

It should be acknowledged that there are times when staff need the
opportunity to 'do nothing', and the value of this must be appreciated.
For example, it may be helpful for someone to reflect on a difficult
visit or situation with other members of the team. This not only
benefits the individual but also helps to develop team identity. It
should therefore be viewed as productive within the culture of the
team rather than as wasted time. Another example is the cup of tea
together first thing in the morning, when the team's energies are
renewed in an informal way. This can be seen as time wasted or merely
as a social activity which delays the start of the real working day. The
legitimacy of reading books and journals within work time and in the
workplace should also be acknowledged. This will avoid the situation
of someone reading, a manager or other colleague walking in, and the
book being furtively and quickly pushed under the desk while the
worker desperately tries to minimise a guilty look.

Allocating resources

Managers constantly are having to make decisions about allocating the
resources at their disposal, usually when demand exceeds supply. In
doing this, a first principle should be to work out solutions in
partnership with users and staff, rather than to adhere rigidly to an
inflexible policy more concerned with rationing than enabling.

Managers have to challenge established practices and orthodoxies
when faced with the typical response 'this has always been the way it
has been done'. Too frequently the only objective is to ensure that
resources are seen to be adequately used, so that their existence is
justified and their future assured. For example, many officers in
charge become very defensive if their units are underoccupied as this
poses a challenge to the future of the establishment. Managers can
look at underoccupancy and question the need for a resource, rather

than query allocation procedures or working practices.

Many factors need to be taken into consideration in deciding how to allocate scarce resources. For example, when there are a limited number of home-help hours, is it better to ensure that a large number of people get a small number of hours or vice versa? Although the emphasis of the 'Caring for People' White Paper (1989) undoubtedly recommends the latter, managers need to be clear not only of their view of what the service is trying to achieve but also aware of the other pressures that may be on them (eg from local politicians who cherish the home-help service). It may appear a straightforward decision to target home-help hours on the more vulnerable, dependent, elderly people in the community in order to achieve the objective of providing an alternative to residential care. Such a course of action is not always straightforward, particularly if local councillors are mobilised against it. The lesson here is for managers to have as wide an appreciation as possible of the various implications of any significant change in the way resources are allocated, and to prepare all those involved, hopefully securing their agreement to a particular solution.

Premises

Important resources of any social services organisation are the premises. These can be of major significance, especially in areas deprived of many facilities. Managers have the opportunity to encourage people to make rooms available to voluntary groups and local people. There are often two standard objections to attempts to do this. The first is concern about the ownership and responsibility for the building in the event of damage or misuse. There may be local authority regulations which make this difficult, problems over insurance, or insufficient money to pay for additional caretaking or cleaning staff. Issues such as these cannot be ignored and sometimes cannot be overcome; however, they should not be regarded as an excuse to prevent any development. Often a 'bit-by-bit' approach can be valuable in proving both the value of such a venture and also that the buildings are still standing afterwards! Objections should not prevent premises being used during normal opening hours by groups which are not run by the organisation's staff, such as mother and toddler groups, self-help groups etc, if the premises are suitable.

The other objection is that residential establishments are 'home' for the people who live there, and that residents are entitled to privacy which maintains their dignity. This view must be respected, but there are ways in which objections can be overcome, for example, by the use of separate entrances, or by involving the residents in whatever is happening, in ways which increase the quality of their experiences, and provide valuable contact with the world outside their home.

There are a number of principles which can be applied when allocating scarce resources. One is to ensure that responsibility for this is delegated as far down the organisation as possible, so staff have a stake in making decisions. To do this, they require the best possible information, including details of the needs of the consumer and the resources available. Thus, in a situation where there are only a limited number of telephones available under the Chronically Sick and Disabled Persons Act, these can be allocated by each team rather than by sending a whole stack of paper applications to middle managers for a decision. A criticism of team allocation is that it allows managers to abdicate their responsibilities, as they are paid to make such decisions. This criticism ignores the probability that, under such a system, resources will be allocated inappropriately. Also, many more initial applications will be completed than there will ever be telephones: there is no greater waste of resources than the time spent making an application for something that is never likely to be available.

Allocations of scarce day-care or residential resources can also be made through a participative process rather than through a paper exercise. Hopefully, one effect of this is a consensus about who is in the greatest need, and it can also help staff and consumers to understand why they did not get a place and the reasons for this. Residential and day-care staff gain important information about why places are allocated, and learn something about the people concerned. In addition, they will also learn about the demand for, and therefore the value of, what they have to offer.

Bombardment

Constant allocation of scarce resources can lead to a sense of bombardment. In such circumstances, the primary aim becomes survival. Little effective or creative work takes place, as attention is directed towards getting through the current work session. Once the day is over, relief is accompanied by fear and apprehension at having to return the next day. Situations of pressure can be quite exhilarating and produce a flow of adrenalin, but only if they are occasional rather than permanent. The latter merely results in a breakdown in the effectiveness of the service provided by the team and also the functioning of the staff. Managers have a key role in preventing this.

One way to approach a sense of bombardment is for managers to try to create a sense of calm and control. This involves making clear judgements under pressure, and not panicking, which will be communicated to the rest of the team. In a situation where there is constant bombardment, managers set the tone by clearly stating the priorities, discussing them with staff, and also explaining them to consumers. This is particularly important because people, even those in desperate situations, can be more reasonable about delays or even refusal of resources if they understand the reasons for it.

The importance of this control is easily demonstrated. Where a number of teams share a building, there may well be one which always appears to be in the midst of crises, and under great pressure. They will claim that far greater demands are placed on them, which may be so in terms of the number of cases they are dealing with. Closer analysis, however, will reveal that their outcomes are fewer, in spite of their activity. For example, they may have more children in care at any one time, but, over a period, the population does not change. Another team may have fewer children in care but, in time, will have rehabilitated more of these successfully to their parents, or made their substitute homes permanent. The difference between the teams will almost inevitably be their team manager's practice, in that teams often become merely a reflection of their manager.

If it becomes clear to any manager that the demands made on the staff over a period far outstrip their ability to meet them, then action needs to be taken. The first step is to monitor, quantify and categorise this demand in a way that can be justified and replicated should further evaluation be called. This monitoring should be part of the normal management process of a department so that comparisons can be made and trends identified, but, as this may not happen, managers need to be able to create such a system.

Having done so, the next step in handling team overload is to identify the priorities for the team and how these can be achieved. This task should be shared with staff with managers providing the lead. Perhaps you should not always, thereafter, deal with situations of need in the rank order of priority, as staff will need variety and a break from high-risk situations.

Priorities need to be recorded formally so that staff know where they stand, and so that middle and senior managers are aware of the position in order to respond to it. Ultimately overload may need to be brought to the attention of senior politicians. Thus team monitoring and prioritising become the first stages in a 'bottom-up' planning process.

Evaluating impact

An important part of managing resources is constant evaluation of the effectiveness of services you are responsible for. Although an obvious statement, it is a task that is often neglected. In the dynamic environment of the personal social services, demands forever are changing, so therefore evaluation has to be ongoing.

Any evaluation of impact must begin by comparing outcome with established aims and objectives and, in doing so, the views of staff and service users need to be sought. Mechanisms need to be agreed so that both groups have a real voice and know that this is taken seriously, and is not merely a token exercise, however uncomfortable this may be for managers.

Evaluating impact is only the first stage of the process, as it is valueless if not accompanied by action. It may confirm merely that current activities are satisfactory and that only minor adjustments need to be made but, more likely, changes will be required. These may be organisational, such as the way in which referrals are allocated, how they are dealt with administratively, and when cases are regarded as legitimately requiring a home visit. More profound policy change may be required, such as an alteration in the opening hours of a day centre to evenings and weekends, generally the most stressful period for carers. Decisions about this fall outside the remit of first-line managers, who need to inform more senior staff of their conclusions, and to report the outcome of these discussions to their staff and service users.

Similarly, if the evaluation demonstrates that the team's effectiveness is minimal because of the strains of bombardment, then it is up to the manager to try to provide the necessary leadership to effect change, and to gain the support of staff for this together with the blessing of senior/middle managers. This is clearly easier to say here than to achieve, yet managers must always be aware that their role is not merely to effect the best allocation of scarce resources but to point out deficiencies, and attempt to create additional resources and new ways of meeting need.

4 Managing conflict

The environment in which managers operate, by its nature, contains conflict. Conflict is evident in all organisations, and managers need to recognise this as a fact of their working lives. In acknowledging the inevitable presence of conflict, the newly appointed manager has taken the first step in becoming comfortable with it. It is a mistake to think that, once current issues are resolved, the once troubled waters will remain smooth thereafter. Conflict is likely to be found in a number of different situations simultaneously, many of which will require positive intervention. Managing conflict can take a personal toll, as it can produce personal dilemmas possibly to the extent that continuing as a manager becomes an issue. There are techniques to deal with this which will be discussed below.

The need for openness

If conflict remains simmering constantly under the surface, it soon becomes the main focus of all conversation and activity, drawing attention away from the tasks in hand. It can also divide teams, as people take sides or form alliances, with the result that staff can lose confidence in the manager's ability to deal with the situation. This lack of confidence well may spill over into the wider perception of the manager's ability.

If the staff group is open and participative, and recognises conflict as normal, then, whatever the reason for disagreement, it can be brought into the open and discussed. Prior to such a discussion, careful preparation is necessary, and managers need a strategy in advance for dealing with the various outcomes which are possible. Discussion may not need to involve all team members, and it is part of the manager's responsibility to decide who needs to be involved. Care also needs to be taken to ensure that discussions are kept to the point and do not degenerate into personal abuse. It is important to ensure that other issues are not introduced, which are not strictly relevant to the matter in hand. There are staff who enjoy seeing people in uncomfortable situations, particularly their manager, and they will take the opportunity to manipulate the situation to their advantage, to have some 'sport'. Managers need to be prepared to face such situations by challenging 'mischief makers', in front of the group if necessary, and being firm about their own position.

The purpose of getting issues out into the open is not only to limit the negative effect of unaddressed conflict, but to arrive at a clear, and hopefully agreed, definition of the problem. It is only when this has been done that there can be any move towards a resolution. The importance of this stage cannot be overemphasised. Those involved may not, at the outset, be talking about the same thing, nor may the first solutions offered be relevant. One example of this was when a team had the opportunity to move out of the main council offices on to one of the estates which they served. Most team members were opposed to this and argued that it would not provide a better service as it would be less accessible to local people: they said so because they were currently close to the main Post Office, DSS and shopping centre. This was a plausible, if slightly dubious, argument, and detailed discussion revealed that they were concerned about their personal safety, in an area with a low level of income, and also the loss of many conveniences for them as staff. There was also a reluctance to take on the responsibilities associated with their own building such as key-holding. The arguments, therefore, related to their personal needs, rather than to a deterioration in the service, and, once this was explicit, it became easier to look for a solution.

If 'solutions' are produced without open debate and clarification of issues, their chance of successful introduction is minimal. Being a manager does not require you to have the answers (to conflicts) in advance without first raising the questions. There may be occasions when some staff are criticised for the work of a colleague in relation to a particular family. This criticism may, in fact, not be specifically about one case but rather be indicative of wider team under-performance and underfunctioning in their work, so that resolving the specific family-related difficulty will not reduce the team's feelings of resentment and hostility about failure to do work properly. Nor would the difficulties created within the team be resolved.

Engaging the conflict

If identifying the elements of any difficult situation is the first and crucial step, in searching for solutions it is important to ensure that there are mechanisms through which staff are able to save face. If someone feels humiliated by the process, this will merely replace conflict with resentment. It can be difficult for people to admit they are wrong and have made a mistake but this is easier if it is part of the culture of the team. As a manager, you too are not infallible and often the team may be right and you wrong. Admit this when it happens, and you will not only gain respect but you will make it easier for other staff to do the same.

An attempt to resolve conflict may be daunting to a new manager. This is particularly so as the situation may well worsen in the short term even when the final outcome is an improvement. When this two-stage process has happened a few times, it gives managers the confidence to face up to such situations in the future. With this comes the ability to back your own judgement yet avoid the danger of arrogance. When you look back, you will think of instances when you went against what you had decided because of pressure from others, yet events proved your judgement to have been correct. When such situations are analysed, you will see it is often the most controversial decisions which are avoided.

For example, during a reorganisation it was agreed to change the membership of the team in order to emphasise that a new structure also required revised working practices. There was strong opposition to this, so the changes were not as extensive as first planned. Reviewing the situation some time later, many of those who opposed the action not only agreed it was beneficial but regretted that it was reduced in scale. It is part of the manager's role to think in the long term while sustaining short-term difficulties.

It is helpful to remember that situations within teams do not remain static, and resolving conflict is likely to create a new set of team dynamics which will help the team to work together more effectively.

Conflict between whom?

The range of people with whom managers can, at some time, come into conflict is enormous, indicative of the complex nature of the task they are faced with. This can include members of the team, colleagues from other parts of the organisation, representative groups, other agencies, the public or other interested parties.

Within the team there can be both personal and professional conflicts between staff. One example of the former is when staff borrow money from each other and then fail to repay it. This may sound trivial but can lead to real difficulties within a staff group, can cause people to take sides, and can have implications for the effective delivery of service. A team manager can take the view that such incidents are technically nothing to do with work and rationalise a strategy of non-intervention, with very damaging consequences. Whilst issues appear minor and insignificant, their potential for ripple effects make them something which cannot be ignored.

In dealing with conflict within the team, it is important to make a conscious effort not to side disproportionately with the more popular or higher status members of the team, or you will be accused of having your own clique, thereby reducing the overall effectiveness of the team.

There will be occasions when managers find themselves in conflict with everyone in the team. This can be when they have made difficult decisions which the team is unhappy with or when they are trying to implement departmental policy which staff disagree with, for example, changes in procedures or reductions in services. Such periods can be very lonely for first-line managers, particularly those newly appointed. Managers need personal strength and support mechanisms to live through such periods, which can be personally very stressful. Support should be present through group meetings, internal alliances with people on the same level, and through formal supervision from your line manager.

Equally, there can be occasions when the team, including the first-line manager, closes ranks in opposition to decisions made by senior managers. This is common when first-line managers do not experience adequate support from their own line managers. The consequences of this are not always constructive, although they can have the effect of improving team identity. One of the dangers of this circumstance is to turn the team against the wider organisation and vice versa, creating dangerous isolation. In addition, when managers inevitably need to exercise authority over their team members on a subsequent issue, this will be more difficult.

A more formal scenario, in which conflict is a regular feature, is the relationship with trade unions. First-line managers can be helped to understand this relationship via induction personnel training. Most disputes concern individual grievances and disciplinary issues rather than the more public national dispute. When members of staff consider they are being treated unfairly, or when new practices are being introduced, the trade union voice may be heard. Positive relationships with the unions is a constructive way of making progress, to the mutual benefit of all parties. Conflict, however, is inevitable at times and managers need to be prepared for this. This can also bring into question the manager's membership of the trade union, as it can produce a conflict of loyalties which some staff may be keen to exploit. Ultimately, no guidance can be issued on this, it is something everyone has to work out personally, but it is helpful to be clear beforehand where you stand rather than be caught unawares during a particular incident.

Conflict of loyalties may also arise when there is disciplinary action taken against a team member, and other staff are called to give evidence about them. This is stressful for everyone, and the consequences can last for some time, not least because those concerned generally have to work together again in the future.

A potential area of conflict exists between the functional groups within a social services department. Fieldworkers can be accused of not understanding the different pressures and difficulties of residential workers or administrative staff and vice versa. Frequently, false assumptions are made about colleagues' attitudes, their role in the organisation and also the importance of particular aspects of their job. Facilitating mutual understanding is critical in order to avoid views becoming entrenched. One way of tackling this is to ensure that staff at all levels have the opportunity to meet with, and understand, the work of colleagues in different work settings. This may sound a simplistic and obvious solution but in practice is surprisingly rare. Ways of achieving this include exchange days, lunches and joint team meetings, which need to take place regularly rather than as one-off events, so that understanding is continually restored, and newly appointed staff are involved.

Not all conflict is within your own organisation. There will be many occasions when there are difficulties with other departments or agencies, over a variety of issues. It is important to remember that conflict is easier to manage in the context of longer-term relationships where openness and honesty are encouraged. This emphasises the value of developing good links with people with whom you come into contact, eg housing staff, teachers, health visitors, doctors, etc. It is inevitable that there will be disagreements, but, if these take place in the wider context of understanding and respect for each other's work, there are fewer dangers of damaging consequences.

Teams, and team members can be, and often are, in conflict with the public. This is common when action is required which involves deprivation of liberty, eg child protection/mental health admissions. One of the roles of a manager in this situation is to provide adequate support to staff which can include face-to-face contacts with the client and/or carers concerned. For example, in child protection work it is important for families to understand that the individual social worker does not carry sole responsibility for decisions that are made, but is part of a corporate body. This both provides the worker with support and honestly represents the situation. In many departments it is the manager, together with the social worker, who explains to families such decisions and the reasons for them.

It is inevitable that staff have to inform people that they are unable to have services which they request or require from the agency. It can help if people are made aware of the reasons for this. It may be because of inadequate or reduced funding, or because applicants do not meet the criteria agreed either by a local authority or by central government. It is useful to have guidelines on criteria publicly available so that it can be made clear that a decision that has been taken is not arbitrary but rather that it is tied to a defined policy that has been adhered to. Conflict over issues such as this can be formalised through an official complaints procedure which can be publicly available. This can depersonalise many issues, and places the manager within a secure structure which makes complaints easier to deal with.

Increasingly, conflict places staff in positions where they are in physical danger from the public, including assaults in offices, people's homes, or residential or day-care establishments. This is an ever-present fear for many staff. Managers can ensure that there is a culture within which both fear of, and actual, assaults are not seen as a consequence of the worker's own inadequacy. It is also important for managers to ensure that staff are trained adequately in aspects of dealing with potentially violent situations.

Managers can take a proactive role with the public in order to reduce the potential for conflict. A good example of this is the development of ordinary living situations as part of 'Care in the Community' initiatives. A small children's home which had been vacant for some time was to become a hostel for people from a long-stay hospital which was closing. A planning application was not well worded and produced considerable local opposition to the project with the usual petitions. All staff involved in planning the change of use, and social workers from the local team, visited all the houses in the vicinity and met others who had signed the petition. They explained what was to happen, left a factsheet and provided the opportunity for local people to visit a similar hostel a few miles away. As a result, opposition turned to support from the majority of local people whose fears were allayed, and who could also see the advantages of the building being occupied again. The lesson learned is the need to carry out a similar exercise before letters are sent out as part of a planning application, and this is now part of the regular consultation process for all developments. The level of conflict about such proposals, while not disappearing entirely, certainly has been reduced.

Action summary: a checklist

Identifying conflict

Managers need to develop appropriate tactics to identify the source of conflict. Can you:

- help those involved to define the issues clearly so that confusion is avoided? This is important, as any solution must resolve the fundamental rather than the peripheral aspects of the problem.

- identify who is affected by the problem, and draw them into the process of finding the solution(s)?
- identify who holds the power in the situation, as they need to be the target for the solutions?
- openly share the analysis with all those involved, in order that people can agree what the problem is, and take ownership of the solution.

Leadership in managing conflict

This involves:

- enabling open discussion to take place about all aspects of the problem, and ensuring solutions are offered.
- avoiding favouritism which sides consistently with the more powerful or higher status members of the team.
- providing direction for staff particularly if the problem appears to be insoluble.
- discussing the situation and possible solutions with your own manager.
- making clear statements to all those involved so that everyone receives and understands the same message. People need to identify the implications for themselves. Remember: do not try to be all things to all people, as this will never succeed and will only give the impression of indecision and vagueness.
- listening to the arguments that are put forward to explain the situation. It is dangerous to prejudge issues, in the light of previous experience, as each situation needs to be considered afresh, and decisions made on the merits of that particular situation.

Solutions

Managers need to be able to offer solutions for the resolution of conflict, although they need to guard against viewing themselves as the font of all wisdom.

- Solutions should emerge from discussions which take place

about the situation and on the basis of the best possible information. But open discussion should not be regarded as a pretext for indecision, and a time limit needs to be established within which proposals become available.

- It is important that decisions are made clearly so that everyone understands the future course of action.
- In proposing solutions, managers need to consider carefully the long-term implications of any course of action. Good solutions may, in many instances, make the situation worse in the short term.
- The reasons for any decisions need to be clearly explained to all concerned, as this should help people accept things which they are initially unhappy about.
- Avoid humiliation for staff who are 'losers'. This involves the provision of 'face savers' which are important for people's own personal status, but also minimise the changes of a division within teams.
- Make every effort to ensure consistency with the general practice of the team. People need an element of predictability and find unpalatable decisions easier if they are within a generally agreed framework.
- Constantly review the situation as it is dangerous to assume that things can be resolved very quickly and then forgotten. Return to the discussion, both within team meetings and in personal supervision, to check if the solution is working and things have actually improved. As part of this, you need to check out that the solution has not been merely to introduce another problem, thereby creating tomorrow's conflict.

Conclusion

One of the signs of a good manager is the ability to resolve conflict, and both your own staff and your senior colleagues will judge you by how well you do this. Working in a situation, where there are a number of conflicts you need to deal with simultaneously, is something you will learn to adjust to, and eventually enjoy. It is also something you will better be able to deal with as you gain more experience and learn from your mistakes.

As a manager, it is important to recognise the responsibilities of leadership, acknowledging that good leaders make their decisions not on impulse but on the basis of good preparation. Are you unsure of all the ingredients of any new situation? Do you know what the likely consequences of any decisions are likely to be, together with the timescale for any solution to be effective?

Good managers also know when not to take action, which situations are likely to resolve themselves or diminish in importance as other more significant concerns take over. Not to act, however, needs to be a positive decision rather than the result of apprehension over the possible consequences of doing what you think ought to be done.

In evaluating how you have dealt with conflict, it is important to review the situation both openly with the team and with others involved, and also with your own line manager. This serves the purpose of confirming where the situation has improved, or where further attention may need to be paid.

Part 2
Reflections
on practice

5   The management of change

Change is a major part of a manager's task.

Change has often been regarded as something to be resisted because it cuts across getting the job done. Change goes with 'meetings, bloody meetings' in the minds of many (J. Cleese). But, as a manager, you will have to play a major part in managing change, provoked by others and initiated by yourself, constantly to improve the quality of work done by your team.

The change phenomenon

It is important for the new manager to recognise that change goes on all the time because of external or internal factors or both. The social services team is always likely to be replacing members or taking on new tasks (internal changes), or absorbing new legislation or departmental procedures (external changes). If a manager can regard change as an opportunity rather than as an obstruction, as something which enhances the quality of the service, it becomes a welcome challenge.

Managers need to appreciate that they can help their teams identify where they can influence change, and are also the key co-ordinators of widely differing perceptions of what is appropriate change. If teams drift into the passive mental set which says 'we can't do anything because x is about to change', low morale based on a sense of powerlessness, will result.

Sometimes it seems that change has been set in motion for its own sake, especially when it is not linked to specific targets, or related to consequences. Change occurs constantly owing to complex activities beyond any one person's or organisation's control. Managers should have a good reason for introducing change. Change should always be purposeful, but it may not be popular. Unpopularity can be minimised by openness and by negotiation between the change agent and those on the receiving end, in order to enhance understanding and involvement.

What triggers change?
It may be helpful for a new manager to have a checklist of what triggers change in the work setting — without such awareness it is all too easy to lose marginality, being overtaken as the sea of change flows forward.
Reactive triggers
Legal changes
Codes of practice
Departmental procedures/guidelines
Changes in principles of good practice
Failure to meet targets, eg not allocating all referrals that require it
Lack of or, alternatively, new resources
Undervaluing the skills of staff
Staff turnover/shortages
Expectations of external agencies/members of the public, eg after a child death inquiry
Technological advances
Changes in demographic patterns
Financial constraints.
Proactive triggers
Drawing up area team profiles
Developing a new vision of practice
Identification of hidden needs, eg child sex abuse
Development of new methodologies, eg networking
Intention to improve service through user consultation.

In community social work settings, the change agent is often the team leader, whether by choice or not.

There are two levels of change in organisations: first-order and second-order. In order to manage change, this provides a useful framework within which to consider what type of change is occurring and/or is appropriate. The team manager telling his/her staff that the hierarchy will be flattened would be a second-order change. However, if one argues that the team manager has used an hierarchical relationship to command this, it would be a first-order change, there being no evidence of actual change in team relationships. In order for it to become a second-order change, which might be required to be effective, the way in which the decision is made would need to be changed. So the team manager would need to engage staff in discussions about the relationships within the team which could lead to a shift in the relationship between team members evident in a flattened hierarchy.

It is easy to be enticed into an illusion that change has occurred. During the 1980s, the decentralisation of the personal social services received extensive coverage. It was believed that decentralisation could improve public access to service and create a more effective match between local need and the resources provided. The focus for change was on organisational structures and office location, and little or no attention was paid to the need to change attitudes, values, perceptions of clients and their contacts.

Change was treated as first-order change with other agency staff when, to be comprehensively successful, it required a second-order change. Decentralisation did not, in fact, change practice and the relationships between staff and public. Improvements, in practice, were dependent largely upon the vision of individual practitioners and managers. To recognise and manage second-order change means dealing with risk and uncertainty.

Second-order change may require illogical jumps from one form of development to another. For example, we persist in adding more and more rules and regulations to the way in which people undertake child protection work in an attempt to improve the protection of children. But changing the rules leaves the way in which agencies relate to each other and attitudes to parents untouched. Children are registered because rules make the net ever wider. It may appear illogical but be essential, to jump from this treadmill reaction to children in need, to stopping child protection conferences and registers, accepting that they actually do not protect children and pay more attention to developing knowledge and relationships outside this ritualised format.

Resource implications

Change may have resource implications which should be built into the strategy for change. It is possible to be more creative about resource development at team level. One team in an urban authority was relocated on to its patch. There was a high incidence of referral and a low level of resources. Through negotiation within the agency, with other agencies and with local people, new resources emerged including a community centre and an ethnic catering service.

If change is viewed as a window of opportunity anything is possible!

Involving staff

If an agency has a tradition of not involving staff in decision-making, it will be difficult for staff to feel positive and involved in the process of change or its intended outcome. The lack of ownership could lead to resistance.

A mere managerial declaration is not enough to make change happen. The manager may think the problem which created the change has been solved but the staff may fail to implement it, they may implement it incorrectly, or even sabotage the solution. This is not managing change, it is merely stating what should happen.

In one local authority, the director decided to reorganise the department. This decision was expressed to the staff six months after his appointment. He said, 'this is how it can be' not 'how should we be organised?'. The staff resisted his vision which ignored their existing commitments and accorded no value to their views. His enthusiasm, in effect, prevented a shared approach to change. The final straw was when he was asked how he had come to his decision. He said he had thought it up on a train journey. The result was disastrous. The rate of staff turnover rose significantly, and the deadline for change slipped constantly. The valuable dimensions to the proposed change were undermined constantly.

It is experiences such as these which deter staff from welcoming change as a worthwhile activity, or from feeling any sense of participation in it. Participation takes time to achieve, but its benefits in the long term will be great. In one local authority, the introduction of the Mental Health Act was seen as likely to undermine the existing generic teams who practised a community-based model, as it required the development of specialist expertise. Through discussion within teams it proved possible to develop a matrix structure which maintained a constructive interweaving of genericism and specialism rather than seeing them as incompatible alternatives. In building up effective aftercare plans for people with mental health problems, approved social workers in mental health were able to use the information held by the community-based teams about local people and potential local support.

For staff to experience a sense of sharing in what will be continuous change, they need to be offered options, not presented with absolutes. For change in practice or policy to be implemented successfully, those directly involved need to own that change, and this can only be achieved through negotiation, be that with staff or public. Once systems to incorporate staff in planning and preparing for change are in place, then, just as change is a constant, so also can be participation.

Not all changes are negotiable, because those brought about by such events as budget reductions or aspects of government policy limit a team's room to manoeuvre. The task of manager is then to identify what is negotiable within the prescribed framework, thus seeking to keep hold of the team's investment in outcome.

Fitting the means to the end

Working methods should be consistent with long-term goals. A manager who does not have regular sessions with staff or who is never seen 'managing by walking about the building' (Peters, 1982) would not have much legitimacy if s/he tried to encourage staff to listen to the local public, for instance. The parallel we would all be familiar with is the parent who shouts, 'will you two stop shouting?' If you cannot think through a way of processing the change which is consistent with the intended outcome, then it will be much more difficult for those who are a part of the process, but who may not hold your vision of the outcome, to become owner/participants.

Where changes in which the team is involved are in contradiction with each other, then reference back to the purpose of the organisation and its mission statement may need to be made. For example, offices opening from 9 am to 5 pm may be inconsistent with the identified needs of a particular group who are only around after 6 pm. If they are the main client group of the agency, then the opening times will need to be changed.

The manager's position in change

The manager will have a leadership role in change. This does not mean necessarily that the manager is the initiator, but it may involve judging a good idea and supporting staff towards its achievement. One team wanted to make their duty service more accessible to their locality several miles away. Team members negotiated venues and information technology equipment. The team manager did the negotiating with the area management group who were resistant to change. This involved placating the management group who wanted a duty officer to be in the area office 'just in case'. In order to free the team to experiment with their planned change, the team manager had to 'cover' the area office. After a short period, the public adjusted and the local people's needs for an accessible service went a step nearer being met.

The manager thus participates in change but also has a place in leading, either from behind or from the front.

The new manager may, at first, seek to meet senior managers' expectations for change such as 'sort out that difficult team member' or 'get the team to change its way of working.' Soon, the team manager will bring personal ideas to influence the new working situation.

Marginality

To be an effective manager, you have to get in and work alongside people, learning to hear what is being said to you. Being a team manager does not place you outside the team. You are, first and foremost, a team member, but you have a different function as a manager. You have one foot in and one foot out. It is the same with a good practitioner who must be involved with, and simultaneously marginal to, local people. Without marginality, there is a risk of becoming part of the problem, or of colluding with the culture, and that would cloud your vision of the ways of achieving change. An effective manager needs to think outside the situation, whilst acting within it.

Stress

Stress will be an issue for managers whose marginality leaves them feeling caught between senior managers and their own staff. Increased personal confidence, personal support systems from within, and outside, the organisation will be important mechanisms for survival.

Using a fallback

It is much easier to identify the changes needed than to achieve them! There will be difficulties *en route*. There is a danger of falling back too heavily on old ways because they are familiar and comfortable and do not demand a great deal of energy or thinking. But for the hard-pressed or stressed manager, a limited amount of fallback may be a necessary safety valve. This should be a planned part of the strategy for change.

However, using a fallback unwisely could mean that a great deal of the momentum for change would be lost. A manager, trying to make his staff more accountable and free to make decisions, reverted to the previous controlling management style when a staff member was found to have committed a fraud, which caused some political embarrassment. The manager began asserting that a supervisory and rigidly hierarchical system was best after all. Rather than viewing this kind of incident as an inevitable risk of change — recognising that some will exploit freedom — a rapid entrenchment took place. Those who were putting their toes in the water were left feeling very unsure, and those who had never wanted to learn to swim anyway exploited the situation to their advantage.

The internal consultant   The manager is ideally placed to be the internal change agent (Schein). Managers have more control over the use of time to plan and devise common goals and can endorse the action for change. However, they have to be sure to set the boundaries between aiding the process of change as a consultant and being the responsible and accountable manager within the organisation. To achieve success requires considerable confidence in oneself and willingness to take risks which may make it difficult in the early days of management.

Ways of aiding change in teams

1 Data collection

According to the task either soft or hard (statistical) data may be more appropriate. Soft data, obtained by talking to people about their views and expectations both inside and outside of the work group will be essential in an analysis of needs and resources, although it takes more time to obtain and analyse the information.

Hard data may be needed when gathering information about the number of callers and the types of information they request, in order to make a case for change. For example, a team developed a new referral form which was computer coded.

The results showed that 70% of their work required skills in debt counselling. A skills inventory showed that they did not possess them. Change was required, and with substantiating figures, a change in posts could be negotiated.

It is important to feed back the results of data collection to staff in order to engage them in the action for change. If the results are available only to management, the team will be left feeling cheated and exploited, and will have more motivation to sabotage than to implement changes. In this instance, the change meant losing 50% of a social work post in favour of a financial information officer. Without staff participation and understanding, based on knowledge of the process and outcome of investigating referrals, a major staff/management confrontation could have occurred.

2 Team building

As a technique for change among staff, team building will help members learn about each other and develop the team culture. The culture is the collection of myths and rituals, values and attitudes that influence activity. An awareness of culture helps identify the need for change, perhaps in attitudes, plans or in corporate action, and places the proposed change in context.

Social services are no exception to the rule that 'the whole is greater than the sum of the parts'. Team building will therefore benefit all work, including making the process of change more effective.

Team relationships are likely to be the first area of change you will have to manage. The mere fact of your own entry into the team will mean change. Whilst the remainder of the members may be unchanged, the whole is an interconnected system. The change of one part will inevitably affect all others. As a new manager, you would be that part.

Incentives to change may be required in some of the more intransigent teams and organisations. It is within the power of a (new) team manager to create or stage-manage rewards at low cost. They will be most effective when closely linked to the positive shifts the team is making towards the agreed aims. Team-building can include conscious enhancement of individual skills, leading to an enhanced career appraisal. To appeal to the child in all of us, rewards can even take the form of cakes at a team meeting and leaving early. Valuing colleagues' worth is essential to managing change.

More detailed exercises can be used by managers, and their teams, to build working relationships. These may be identifying and building aims together, undertaking an area profile together or clarifying and optimising the value of differences (Hearn and Thomson, 1987). It may be helpful to identify the assumptions which underlie a manager's approach to team work.

A sample set of assumptions

1. A work group cannot be defined as a team unless the members are interdependent.
2. Teams will establish explicit and shared goals which will become their team working contract.
3. Team members need to define activities together, based on agreed goals and objectives.
4. Once the goals and tasks are set, the team needs to develop processes for communication, decision-making and conflict management.
5. The team will require mechanisms whereby they can work out interpersonal issues brought about by interacting in the work setting and be able to integrate their experiences from outside with the internal system.

An external consultant   As suggested earlier, change may be unwanted, complex and may require skills not held within the team. To introduce a person from outside the organisation provides objectivity. A consultant should have credibility and possess skills in the process of change: it is not necessary to have expertise in the intended outcome, though this can enhance the consultancy. The choice of consultant should be negotiated with the group. Funds may have to be made available from budgets normally used for other things.

Dealing with resistance

What is the cause of resistance to change?
Experience shows that resistance can be due to:

1. A sense of uncertainty which results from lack of information as plans develop.
2. Habit and inertia — 'it's always been like this' syndrome.
3. Unwillingness to cut losses that is: 'we've made an investment in *x* we must carry on and not face *y*'.
4. A dilution of status/power for some, whether staff or politicians, perhaps because a coalition will be disrupted.
5. A loss of contact, eg colleagues, a neighbourhood.
6. Resource implications, if change is perceived as reducing resources or requiring more staff.
7. Lack of understanding, eg of new ideas.
8. Conflicting values and beliefs. For example, the 'carer of people' may resist what is seen as a more competitive service environment.

Resistance may be overcome in several ways.

1. Helping staff to identify the links between past and present activity.
2. Setting up training programmes to aid the development or/and mastering of skills.
3. Opening up discussions with those who have initiated the change(s) and those on the receiving end.
4. Making it safe to take risks.
5. Checking out with service recipients that the changes planned are seen as offering them a better service.
6. Appointing new staff. At the bottom line, staff may need to change. Those who wish to work as therapeutic social workers may not be able to stay in a department or agency where the

focus is on service delivery.
7. Creating new networks of support where new skills are reinforced.

If none of these methods works you may have to take the decision to stop investing in a loser rather than expecting staff to carry the decision.

Networks and teams

People are not only parts of a team but also of a range of interconnected work-related systems — or networks. It is important to evaluate the ripple effects of change through these networks. The team may decide, for example, to put proportionally more effort into work with vulnerable elderly people. If, in this instance, a worker is moved into this work who had expertise and a significant consumer network around work with adolescents, then the relations with the youth and community in the locality will deteriorate and the worker may even leave.

Analysing the networks

Because networks are complex you have to be in post for a while before you can understand the significance of different patterns of internal relationships, and also external patterns involving competitors, collaborators and customers. Some internal networks will be a mix of personal and work relationships, for example, a colleague may also be a boyfriend. Some will have a limited task focus, like a project group, and others will be prescribed by procedures such as child protection work, as well as the more obvious organisationally led network of the area office or residential home. Some will be permanent and some transient.

There may be overlaps between networks, it is possible for conflicts between networks to be held within the one person. A practitioner developing local networks in a neighbourhood may find that connections with one set of people, for example, adolescents, can cause problems when associating with another such as frail elderly people. The team leader often plays a valuable role in helping staff to become bridges between factions rather than colluding with the conflict.

Overlap between internal networkers may also cause divided loyalties. Your team may claim more work than any other which leads to a competitive bid for a restricted new resource. You may request data from your team member, one of whom is married to a member of another competing team. The effect of domestic debate has to be taken into consideration when planning the strategy. Loyalties have to be established and ground rules set for how people participate in the process of change. Some may be more active than others, inequity of action should not get translated into negative back-biting. Holding people together means helping them to value each other, even to value their differences.

Evaluation

An important component of change, which can confirm and reinforce growth, is careful monitoring and evaluation. Looked at another way, assessment of change will reduce accusations that they were introduced for their own sake, or were driven by ego, it is commonly said that new directors announce their arrival by restructuring!

1. Audit approach

Draw staff together at regular intervals and ask them to make a presentation on the effect of the changes, and assess the advantages and disadvantages of the outcomes intended when the change was originally agreed. It is informal and subjective but ensures that staff focus on evaluating the whole by listening to each other. It may be that presentations are given by some of the recipients rather than by the in-house staff.

2. Gathering of anecdotes

Telling positive stories about the changes as they develop can help to establish them. This is an even more informal approach and can create the by-product of new myths and rituals: these reinforce the new culture developing with the changes.

3. Research and development approach

Ask the consumers what they feel about the changes. Care is needed in interpreting responses. For example, one locally based team working to make people less dependent on their social work aides and to integrate with the local caring networks, asked its old customers their views. They thought the new service was dreadful, as they liked the weekly chat with the social work aide. However, new customers, who had not been in the system before, liked the greater choice and sense of control over the help that they received. The two sets of findings required different interpretations.

4. Pilot assessing

When a change can start with a pilot, and then be introduced in stages, then it is worthwhile evaluating it at each stage and reassessing strategy before moving on.

Conclusion

As a manager of change, you need to recognise and acknowledge feelings, both your own and those of the other people involved in the process of change. Get a taste of their view of the world and try and interweave it with your own. Change involves turbulence: breaking old relationships, replacing the known with the unknown, and changing skills can be painful. Managing resistance to change requires both acknowledgement of 'loss' and feelings of grief, and also attention to participative planning, negotiating and anticipation of the consequences of changes.

Do not try to make major changes too soon after your arrival. Changes that are being shouted for by all are the ones that a new manager should focus upon first, even if they will have minimal impact on the wider organisation or the consumer. A small success will raise your credibility with those you manage and set a good foundation for the changes yet to come. Remember to pace yourself, use supervision and take time off for personal review!

References
Cleese, J. Meeting Bloody Meetings, BBC Video.
Peters and Waterman (1982). *In Search of Excellence*, Harper & Row.
Schein (1987). *Process consultation*, Addison Wesley.
Hearn and Thomson (1987). *Developing Community Social Work in Teams*, National Institute for Social Work.

6 Managing risk

Every day of their working lives, social services workers deal with members of the public who are at some degree of risk. By its nature, social work is concerned with helping those who are vulnerable, ranging from elderly people neglecting themselves to children at risk of abuse by their parents or by others. A community social work approach involves professionals working in partnership with people in neighbourhoods and other communities to protect vulnerable people. Practitioners believe that the 'professional care system' cannot, by itself, protect people and point out several apparent failures of social services departments to do so. It is argued that people in neighbourhoods or in other communities can, in effect, be galvanised or persuaded to offer a degree of self-protection over their vulnerable members, and there are examples where this has been done, mostly in the field of adult care.

Community social work practice strives for the empowerment of consumers or clients, and states that, in order to achieve this, professionals have to relinquish their power to define the needs of those whom they serve. This approach has been imparted in some areas with great success.

There is no doubt that the Government's adoption of the broad principles of the Griffiths report in the White Paper 'Caring for People' will move Social Services and Social Work Departments much more towards this way of working in the 1990s.

It is, however, in the area where social services departments have statutory powers and *duties* to protect people that community social work has to withstand the most rigorous test. Above all else, it is the field of child protection in which the efforts of social services departments have been judged in the last 15 years. This chapter will examine the management of risk and will relate this to some of the major aspects of community social work. We argue that there are benefits and limitations to this approach. We will focus on management and not on practice issues in working with risk, and we do not pretend to provide a blueprint for practice, but rather to highlight certain issues for managers.

What is risk?

We are managing the risk to clients caused by their vulnerability, but we can make a distinction between social services' role with vulnerable adults and children. Adults have rights, and one of these is the right to make an informed choice about how to live their lives and whether to accept help. Often our work with vulnerable adults, particularly with confused or mentally ill elderly people, is about protecting their rights to make those choices. It is only when we assess that their ability to make decisions about risk and protection is impaired that we use statutory powers to intervene. Part of managing risk may be to make care arrangements which diminish the risk, but it remains an adult's informed choice, for example, in the case of a frail elderly person who decides to remain at home. This is often an aspect of the community social work role that neighbours or family find hardest to understand: they think we protect adults in the same way as children.

We do not expect children to protect themselves from severe risk or harm. Their legal right *vis à vis* those of their parents are less well defined. We expect adults to protect children, and the law gives powers to statutory agencies to intervene to protect children when they are being insufficiently protected from 'significant' harm (Children Act, 1990). It is this difference in the protective role in the management of risk which has given the protection of children the high profile it has in social services departments and in social workers' daily working concerns.

This difference does not diminish the stress and difficulty of working with other vulnerable groups, but highlights a difference in the statutory role. Community care developments suggest that teams will be working (more) with vulnerable adults at some degree of risk in the community. While we focus here mainly on child protection, the principles established are generally applicable.

Not only are members of the public at risk but so are the organisation and individual members of staff. In chairing a child protection conference, a team manager is working for the department in a risky area. When things go wrong, a department can expect both hostile publicity and criticism which extends to the management of the family. Rosemary Stewart (1976), when analysing the manager's task, comments that the degree of risk to be managed is measured by the extent to which the activity is *visible* and for which the manager is *personally accountable.*

The risks to staff are significant as well. People can experience loss of morale, a sense of failure and paralysis. The physical risk of violence, when working with hostile, unpredictable people, has to be taken into account.

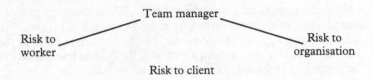

Fig. 6.1 Managing risk

Planning and assessment of risk

Assessment of risk to individuals involves considering many factors which can be expressed along a continuum from low to severe. At points along this continuum, it is necessary to take action. Predictable factors, based on previous behaviour, have a role to play, but are not decisive; the current social and emotional factors are as important.

Managers need to know what they are looking for, and what sort of questions to ask, in order to assess the level of risk. For example:

- has a thorough assessment been made, including care available in the family and local neighbourhood?
- is the child being seen alone and in context?
- are all parties involved working effectively together?

This is as relevant to providing packages of care for vulnerable adults as it is for child protection.

Decisions

In taking decisions, eg about whether to call a case conference, or to take legal steps to remove children, we need to be clear about our reasons, and mindful of the outcome. Decisions are not just about the present: they can vitally affect the future, both for parents and children, with implications for further social work intervention. Case planning via reviews, case conferences, supervision, has to identify the desired outcome, specify the necessary change and tasks to be achieved. Alternatively, we may have to be honest that our goal is maintenance, if change is not possible. Either way, clarity is the key here.

Child protection registers must also be used purposefully if they are to be relevant. Registration can acquire a momentum of its own. Many social workers think that 'it's very easy to get on them, but almost impossible to get off'. During conferences, other concerns about the family can arise which can overtake the original reasons for registration (which may have diminished). These concerns may, or may not, be sufficient reason to keep a child's name on the register. In order to reach appropriate decisions, you need to refer back to the original reason for registration, identifying the current levels of risk in the context of registration criteria and quality of life.

Management of practice

One of the recurring themes of much statutory work with children, including child abuse inquiry reports, has been the standard of management and supervision. In many cases, particularly so in Cleveland, managers failed to grasp the nettle of what was going on, and act. Taking action does not mean charging around in a rather heady and purposeless way. 'Looking busy' is a characteristic of many social services managers but does not mean necessarily that any significant action is being taken. Appropriate action is a product of thought which has been undertaken in a clear, calm way. We must model the approach we require, rather than the client's current behaviour. Workers have to feel confident that they are empowered by managers both to act and to take risks. Staff who feel disabled will probably be unable to do either, so situations will drift. Some have lamented the demise of supervision in a manager's schedule. To lament is not enough. Good supervision is crucial for effective management of risk, as it is in this forum that cases are planned and workers have the opportunity to reflect on their role and intervention in a case. It is also the manager's opportunity to review the work and exercise the objectivity that distance affords him/her.

Managers do not work in a vacuum. Their own supervision and support is crucial to their effective management of risk. Creating good support networks via peers and colleagues assists this, but the main responsibility lies with principal officers to develop and support first-line managers via training and supervision. There is widespread suspicion that planned supervision disappears about one-third of the way up the management structure of many agencies. In one local authority, a public child death inquiry identified lack of supervision of managers as a key issue. External trainers, over three subsequent years, asked each group of team managers they worked with whether they received supervision when they required it. Only one team manager on each course of twelve received it. Many still had received none three years later.

The absence of supervision can reinforce the view that it is unnecessary. It is then difficult to change established practice.

The management of risk relies upon the exercise of judgement. One of the hardest dilemmas for a manager is to decide the degree to which workers should be given discretion to exercise judgement. Part of the task is to enable workers to make judgements and develop skills and confidence to do this via support and constructive criticism. This works well with a competent worker. However, in a situation where such competence is missing, a common solution is to minimise the risk by allocating as few child protection cases as possible to that worker. Whilst fellow team members appreciate this for professional reasons, it is clearly unsatisfactory to distribute the workload unevenly and unfairly. The absence of formal staff development and appraisal procedures in many agencies makes the solution to these problems more difficult.

It can be useful for teams to participate in developing good practice guidelines based on departmental procedures: this stimulates discussion and helps teams to set standards which they can own and achieve.

Partnership

Greater accountability for planning and action are common themes both in the 'Caring For People' White Paper, subsequent legislation and in the Children Act 1989. Local authorities will have to make public community care plans and criteria for assessments. 'Caring for People' stresses the involvement of users and carers in drawing up these plans and devising packages of care. The Children Act makes the local authority more accountable for the use of statutory powers and subsequent action taken and lays great emphasis on working in partnership with parents. The concepts of shared care and partnership are central to the Act's philosophy. The DHSS research 'Decision-making in Child Care' (1986) confirmed that social workers frequently lay insufficient emphasis on finding alternatives to care. The Children Act hopefully will encourage a greater effort to listen to parents and children.

Partnership is also central to the theory and practice of community social work. To what degree can community social work principles be applied to child protection work and managing the risks involved? The majority of the 43,000 children on child protection registers in this country are living within their families or extended families. If we examine the case conference recommendations that lead to registration and the interagency protection plan, the protection of the children in question is frequently entrusted to a group of professionals. Most of these, apart from school teachers and nursery staff, are unlikely to see the child more than once a week. There has to be greater scope for working *with* parents who abuse their children, rather than 'on' them.

One of the main yardsticks by which these attempts of partnership are measured is the degree to which parents are involved in multidisciplinary case conferences. The Department of Health pamphlet 'Working Together' (1991) asks Area Child Protection Committees to involve parents as far as possible. 'Openness and honesty are an important basis on which to build a foundation of understanding and respect between parents and professionals which will often be essential for a satisfactory outcome for the child. Parents views should be sought on the issues to be raised prior to a case conference to afford them the opportunity to seek advice and prepare their point of view. They should be invited to case conferences unless in the view of the chair of the conference their presence — will preclude a full and proper consideration of the child's interests'.

Clearly, the participation of parents in child protection conferences builds on the foundations of other good practice. In several areas, parents are now invited to attend review conferences and, in some areas, to initial conferences as well. The term 'parents' should not be taken too literally. What is meant is the responsible guardian who, in some instances, may be aunt, grandparent, or legal guardian.

For participation to be effective, managers, who are often chairs of conferences, have to ensure that parents are listened to, and given the opportunity to challenge, what is said. Conference participants should continue to exchange information freely and openly. The focus of the conference remains the protection of the child.

It is in cases of severe abuse, where legal action ensues, that the question of parental participation is most difficult. However this is managed, it is preferable that parents have an opportunity to put their views to the conference before final decisions are made. At initial conferences, it is important to be clear about the parents' part in the decisions made, for example, whether the conference excludes the parents, before making decisions about registration.

In most child protection cases, children remain at home, and their main sources of protection are their parents. Plans, constructed at conferences where parents are present and have heard and understood the concerns expressed by workers, are more likely to be owned subsequently by parents. These plans must benefit the child and assist in the task of managing risk.

Partnership implies a degree of equality in the relationship which, once the local authority takes statutory powers, is absent from its relationship with parents. The Children Act 1989 acknowledges this by seeking to make the local authority much more accountable for the way in which these powers are exercised. This absence of equality of power in partnership in no way diminishes the need to work with parents, particularly over questions of access, throughout a child's career in care. The majority of young people re-form relationships with their families upon leaving care. Research has shown that the families of children in care change and reconstitute, and social workers need to work with parents to keep their children in touch with this (Doyle, 1988).

Can people in neighbourhoods and other communities be involved in protecting vulnerable children? Heightening awareness and trying to engage people in some level of dialogue about the statutory duties that social services departments hold is clearly possible, and has been achieved by some teams. In an urban authority, the child abuse review officer and social work team collaborated to research local peoples' views of abuse and child protection. They did this by advertising their interest in the local paper and meeting groups. The outcome over an 18-month period was a roadshow of social workers and local people explaining, to local groups, their joint responsibility to protect children (Doyle, 1988).

A consistent thread coming out of child abuse inquiries of the last 15 years, however, is that parents who seriously abuse their children are frequently socially isolated; the families of Kimberley Carlisle, Tyra Henry and Jasmine Beckford were as remote to their neighbours as they were to the professionals whose roles were to protect these children. There is scope for working in greater collaboration with extended family members in plans to protect children. Trying to involve other people, outside extended families, in protective, supportive and monitoring roles, is much more difficult. The still significant percentage of anonymous referrals to the NSPCC and social services suggest responsible and vigilant attitudes on the part of the public. However, the partnership ends there. Responsibility is still too readily handed over. To enter into open debate and involvement with local people requires a greater knowledge of localities and their norms. It requires a willingness to walk amongst people and talk about the needs in an area. To establish effective relationships in neighbourhoods is the result of slow and persistent work. It will not effect change rapidly enough to help the next child referred but is an essential strategy if the 'us and them' attitude between workers and public is not to persist.

Working together

One of the key themes in all the child abuse inquiries has been the importance of interagency co-operation. Failure to understand each other's role, together with lack of communication and trust, have produced what now seem elementary errors. In recognition of this, one of the most important documents published as a response to the Cleveland Report and subsequently updated is 'Working Together'. This guides interagency co-operation in the protection of children from abuse, and stresses that agencies should develop and agree joint policies, monitor practice and provide joint training. A clear structure for this is provided for via Area Child Protection Committees. As with all structures though, it will only be as effective as its member parts.

At a local level, team managers can develop good working relationships on a person-to-person basis, with staff from other agencies who operate in the same areas. Child protection work should not be a special event for which a group of relative strangers come together. Case conferences are only one aspect of working together, and here the development of confidence and mutual understanding of each other's roles enhances the work. Equally, it is probably better that agencies explain their difficulties, for example, over staff shortages, to each other rather than to retreat into defensive postures. This is just as important at Area Child Protection Committee (ACPC) level as it is at a local team level. ACPCs must be aware of operational realities when making policies.

Many initiatives have been undertaken by community social work teams which demonstrate ways of working together. For example, a schools' liaison project developed out of local primary schools' interest in learning more about working with child sexual abuse. Team members participated in training sessions at three primary schools on 'Baker days' and then became link workers for the schools. Confidence in making referrals and working with social services increased.

Good but not perfect practice

Unpredictability is inherent in risk. Situations where we can be absolutely sure of the outcome are not risky. There is a tendency in social work to aspire to standards which the nature of the task prohibits. We do not always get things right — especially when dealing with the unpredictable behaviour of human beings. The assumption that social workers can prevent all fatal injury to children was firmly squashed by the report into the death of Liam Johnson which identified a 'dangerous assumption — that all violence is predictable and preventable. The reality is very different'. The report finds no evidence of negligent practice or of serious errors of judgement. It is important that social workers and managers do not shoulder responsibility which is not properly theirs.

The comments of this report on the unpredictable nature of child protection work apply generally. 'Children do die, sometimes tragically, and sometimes at the hands of those who should care for them. Responsibility for these deaths lies overwhelmingly with those who kill them, not with those whose role has been to try to help the family'.

Managing uncertain, unpredictable, situations means seeking to diminish the risk as far as possible, assessing both risks and strengths, and monitoring the balance between the two.

The significance of parts of a protection plan not working needs to be understood and contingency plans made. This is true for a child protection plan, a care package for a frail, elderly person, a plan to establish a young adult with learning difficulties in more independent accommodation and a discharge plan from psychiatric hospital.

It is equally important not to lose sight of the many occasions when children are adequately protected through the efforts of parents, family, friends, social workers and other professionals. This also involves taking risks, of the kind which the following example illustrates. A couple, whose first child aged five months had suffered a severe fracture and bruising, gave birth to a second child four years later. It was never known how the first child's injuries had been caused. He was in fact removed on a place of safety order and, after attempts to rehabilitate him at home were unsuccessful, he was placed for adoption. Debate ensued as to whether, given the seriousness of the first child's injuries, the new baby should be placed with foster parents whilst an assessment took place, or whether the baby could be safely left at home during the assessment. The latter course of action was adopted taking into account the baby's age (newborn), the observations of the parents' interaction and handling of him and their increased maturity since the first incident. Further assessment of the parents' subsequent good care of the baby showed this to have been the correct course of action but, nevertheless, there were risks which were acknowledged in the assessment and plan of work with the family.

The effect of gender

Some of the main features of families where children have died have been social isolation, unwillingness or refusal to co-operate with statutory agencies and the intimidation of social workers and other professionals. These families pose some of the most difficult problems for managers. Managing risk also involves managing fear. Nearly all sexual abuse and major physical abuse towards children is perpetrated by men. These men are frequently excluded from the orbit of professional intervention because of three things:

- they choose to exclude themselves.
- early assumptions are made that these men are incapable of significant change in their behaviour, so that professionally focused intervention to help them will be pointless.
- These men frequently are threatening and have been violent towards professional staff.

A number of social work staff have been assaulted in their careers; there can surely be no one who has not felt fear, or who does not regularly feel frightened, at the prospect of visiting particular families. We have to find ways of working with these families whereby we continue to offer a service and protect both client and staff sufficiently. The issues around balancing client needs and staff protection are just as significant in mental health work.

Often our reaction is to exclude people — from offices, from discussions, from visits. In family situations, this places the woman in an almost impossible position where she has the full responsibility for protecting children from a man with whom the statutory agencies refuse to have contact. Frequently, the agency's expectations of women as parents are high and of men are low. The focus of intervention is, therefore, the woman even though the man is nearly always the abuser.

We require women to choose between partners and children, and, in sexual abuse cases, frequently underestimate a woman's shock and denial and misinterpret it as collusion. Following a judgement of collusion, mothers as well as fathers can be denied access: a vivid example was in Cleveland when children were removed to a place of safety.

The fear of violence

Agencies have to confront issues of family violence and unacceptable behaviour towards staff. Planning is crucial to work out how cases will be handled, when and where people will be seen, and how staff will be supported. Staff have to feel able to say when they feel frightened. Care for staff cannot be left out of attention to practice. There is more to staff care than panic buttons and security screens. If the culture of a social work team encompasses an approach to working in partnership with client and neighbours, the team must accommodate the vulnerability that staff may feel at times, out on the street. Managers have a responsibility to ensure that the work environment is supportive and that staff unease and concern can be expressed openly. Managers need to foster a culture where it is okay — sometimes crucial — to feel scared in social work teams. Male managers in particular have a responsibility to challenge the macho-response to issues of staff risk and care.

References

Stewart, R. (1976). *Contrasts in Management*, McGraw Hill.

DHSS (1986). Decision - making in child care, *HMSO*.

Doyle, M. (1988). Child Abuse Action Group report, available, Hammersmith Social Services Department.

7 Building a culture

Why culture?

'Organisation culture', managing the culture, changing the culture, cultures of excellence; these are all phrases which slip easily off the tongues and pens of speakers and writers about management, suggesting that today's manager must have an understanding of organisation culture.

Simple experience and observation also bear this out, although not necessarily in the way that these phrases imply. Any observer of social services departments can testify to the difference in areas, and teams and the effects of these differences on the way social work is practised. Our observer would also comment on the impact of the prevailing culture on workers in an organisation. Researchers into social work teams (Stevenson and Parsloe, 1981) and practice have also noted the importance of teams developing a shared ethos for practice.

Building a culture which sustains team members, encourages an active and consistent response to service users, based on commonly agreed goals, is part of a first-line manager's job. The culture of the organisation and of the team provides the context within which a manager operates, and an understanding of the culture is crucial to team development and the management of change within the organisation. For example, teams and managers wishing to promote antiracist or antisexist policies by recruiting more black workers or job sharers need to understand the impact on individuals of being different from the predominant culture of the organisation, and the expectations that will arise. A culture which sustains and appreciates differences has to develop. It is people's actions and behaviour which will achieve these changes, and managers' skills can enable this.

What is organisational culture?

A review of the literature suggests two main ways in which organisation culture is defined. The first seeks to identify a prevailing culture which encompasses a dominant system of beliefs and values on which the organisation operates. The culture affects the organisation's ability to respond and change, and its management is crucial to effective management of the organisation as a whole. By implication, culture is somewhat separate from the work-a-day structures and processes.

The second identifies culture as the means by which the organisation operates: structures (the way things are ordered) and processes (the way things are done) are important manifestations of the culture. Culture is defined by the way in which members sustain themselves, and the way in which the organisation changes. A culture thus contains the guiding principles and the diversity created by everyday practices and assumptions. The first implies management *of* culture; the second, management *with* (or within) a culture. Which definition is more helpful in understanding the many and varied workings of social services departments?

There is a tendency to see cultures (according to either description) as set at the top, and the role of managers as to carry the culture so that it permeates the whole organisation. In fact, changes in culture can emanate as much from the bottom as from the top. Many teams have developed community social work as a response to service needs and to their own professional philosophy. Projects for parental participation in case conferences have been initiated by social work practitioners. Examples are numerous, and show the prevailing culture having a significant impact on how easy, or difficult, it is for practitioners to develop good practice.

Various different types of organisational cultures have been identified. Charles Handy (1981) and Roger Harrison (1975) have described the following cultures:

Power culture

This is highly centralised, reliant on strong leadership from the top, sometimes benevolent but also autocratic.

Role culture

This is an organisation in which all jobs are well described; people do not deviate from these descriptions; each department works to its own procedures; co-ordinated only at the top.

Task culture

This is a dynamic achievement-orientated culture, which values personal competence and getting the job done.

Person culture

This is a rare form in which individuals have no identification with the organisation's objectives or demands.

All these cultures have advantages and disadvantages. *Role culture* is fair but ponderous and slow to adapt to change; *task culture* is exciting to work in but heavily demanding; *power culture* allows for little questioning or criticism. Different and perhaps incompatible cultures may exist side by side in an organisation, so culture will be experienced variously by its members.

This model is useful in identifying dominant modes of operation which affect an organisation's ability to change. Local authorities and large voluntary organisations most closely correspond to role cultures, hence their difficulty in responding quickly to change. The demands of the present environment with consumer choice and performance-related pay, will alter this, probably towards more task orientation. One of the advantages of role cultures is the existence of policy and guidelines, which, whilst they can be restrictive, are also important in establishing a framework for practice.

Balancing autonomy with the need to maintain central control over key values and functions is a theme of Peters and Waterman (1982). They identified the characteristics of corporate cultures of excellent companies, contending that it was on the strength of these cultures that their excellence was based. Their emphasis on being close to the customer, valuing workers, and enabling experimentation is particularly relevant to managing personal social services agencies.

If culture is primarily about the way in which things are done, then any definition has to take into account the goals, and values and assumptions of all members of the organisation, and the way in which these create the culture and affect the service provided. The complexity of many organisation cultures accounts for the diversity so apparent within social services departments; the varying use between teams, for example, of child protection registers and statutory intervention, or the differing use of neighbourhood and community resources. Culture is one of the means through which members of an organisation give meaning to their task. Policies and guidelines enshrining values and expectations, and a strong team subculture, are part of this.

Culture is the context within which change takes place, provides continuity and strength as much as obstacles to change. As people's behaviour changes, so does the culture.

The existing culture can be a source of change (Marshall and Maclean, 1985). At times of change, staff in an organisation frequently feel undervalued, as if the way they worked before was of no worth. The implementation of the Community Care reforms will require a significant cultural change from provider to needs-led assessment. Some good assessment practice exists in social services departments and is already part of the culture. Valuing work that is being done, and building on the strengths, can be effective ways of working with these aspects of the culture which need to change.

Culture can be affected by individuals. All social services departments provide procedures for the investigation of suspected child abuse: these are important in establishing an interagency framework for the investigation for workers to follow. The service that the client receives reflects not only the agency's procedures, but the worker's own approach, and the way in which such investigations are usually carried out in that team or area. Managers, too, regularly take crucial decisions, about conferencing and taking places of safety, which decisions create a climate in which the work takes place and affect the type of service people receive. The arrival of new managers, taking different sorts of decisions, can change this, and so affect the culture of the area or team.

Organisational culture has many layers. Policies or guidelines, which give meaning or purpose, the senior management style, underlying assumptions about what is important, and about the way things are done, all contribute. The culture reflects both diversity within the organisation, and can provide some continuity at times of change.

Knowing your culture

Think of your first impressions of an organisation you have just joined. What are the jokes and stories? Who are the key people — what are their attitudes and values? Who are significant senior people — their attitudes? Think about the overall culture, statements about purpose. Think about team cultures in the same way. Identify strengths. What is valued? What are the team's goals? Get a sense of the place and build up a picture which will help you to be a manager within it.

Drawing pictures of the culture of an organisation is a powerful way of understanding it. I have done this in workshops with middle managers. One picture depicted current changes as threatening the safety of children, because insufficient emphasis was placed on a current strength in the organisation — its good standards of preventative social work. Another showed the way in which benevolent inaction disempowers managers and thus workers.

Look for symbols of the culture which are important in understanding these cultures. Are there, though, situations where high-profile symbols not borne out in day-to-day work life cause anger and frustration? Are your equal opportunities policies high-profile symbols, and, if so, are they accompanied by action in terms of recruitment and training opportunities? Or, does the culture of the organisation remain the same?

It has been shown (Rothwell, 1985; Davies, 1985) how certain myths and assumptions sustain the dominance of men in senior managerial positions. The myth is of an open, accessible system. However, performance is evaluated on male values, and a career break or a desire to work part-time is seen as detrimental — showing lack of commitment to a career in management or to the organisation. Thus, women either conform or need to find ways of changing these aspects of the organisation's culture. Strategic thinking by women, challenge and mutual support are crucial to this.

Building a culture

There are various ways in which managers' behaviour affects the culture of a team. In a research study of managers' practice, Rosemary Stewart (1976) asserts: 'There is a key difference in approach between the manager who sees the job as primarily *responding to and coping* with problems and requests as they arise, and the one who sees it as operating in an environment inside and where relevant to the job outside, the company (organisation), which she tries to *control, to develop and to mould* as she desires'.

It is common for middle managers (and probably senior managers) in social services to assert that they have little control over what they do. Stewart's model, which is based on a research study of manager's practice, suggests that it is possible for managers to exercise choice and control over their activities. This is crucial to the implementation of change or to the development of innovative practice, and, of course, affects staff.

I once used this quote with a group of newly qualified workers, recently recruited to a hard-pressed department, who were all very keen to practise well-planned preventative social work. Quotes can provide a framework for thinking about the task ahead. To achieve effective preventative work, they would need to control, mould and develop creatively, no longer limited to reactive interventions. The difference in approach is quite fundamental, and depends upon how powerful, or otherwise, we feel in our own world. Managers, like practitioners, have to analyse why they are operating in a certain way before trying to change to a different mode of operating.

What practical benefits derive from an analysis of organisational culture? It provides a framework for understanding the way in which organisations operate, and suggests skills for managing change and developing community-orientated services. The organisation's culture (ie the way people work within it) is the source of the change. In order to change culture, managers have to work with it. Key skills for this are: analysis, listening and valuing, creating frameworks (philosophies and goals), strategic thinking and teamwork.

Managers can target training resources strategically. If you wish to increase the number of black or women managers in an organisation, then management training opportunities should be prioritised accordingly.

The culture forms the base from which people learn new ways of working, and thus the culture changes. In seeking to provide a more responsive, customer-orientated service, managers can work from the basis that staff are interested in providing this sort of service and value efforts already made to do so, rather than impose the change in a way which undervalues staff. In planning a move to a decentralised neighbourhood office, it is as important to identify and value existing skills and links which can be built on, as it is to focus on the ways in which the service delivery will change. If, for example, a team has had good links with home care by virtue of sitting in the next office, it is worth talking to the home care team about how to keep the good links when the team moves. Developing an ethos for the new service (ie a 'what we want to do when we're there') and sharing the tasks are activities which contribute towards people's commitment to the change and to the changes in the culture.

Other aspects of culture building include implementing policies of client access to information, so that recording practice changes and a climate of openness is created, examining how referrals are received and what sort of information is passed on. It is important to be receptive to what consumers say about services and to be ready to act on their comments. As was argued earlier, it is important, too, that social workers have policies and guidelines to provide a framework for practice. Managers have a key role both in writing these and also in their own practice and decision-making. Creating the culture of a responsive service is very much part of the manager's role. Working with teams, establishing principles, tasks and ownership of the service are keys to developing good practice in community social work.

Managers can work with teams to create common aims, and, at the same time, respect difference and diversity, acknowledging both the varied contributions and different sorts of pressures that respective members of the team experience. In this way, team members will share skills 'and learn from each other. Peters and Waterman emphasise tHe necessity of encouraging experimentation from which everyone learns. Failure is seen as a sign of innovation; mistakes can be educational, and individuals are not blamed. In order to take risks and be innovative, staff have to feel secure, and part of the management task is to provide boundaries. Returning to the original models, a blend of role culture (providing procedures and systems) and task culture (ensuring action and some support) would provide this.

At times, teams feel at odds with the culture of the organisation, and, within organisations, there are many subcultures. Many people working in one sort of culture might prefer to work in another, and it is quite possible for managers to build team cultures which reflect both some aspects of the prevailing organisational culture (eg, the core values) and some aspects of their own, the team's preferred culture. Such differences can be challenging for the organisation, and middle managers can experience considerable stress whilst holding the tension between the two cultures. In cultures where the dominant mode of operation is to be cautious and cover your back, managers who allow staff to take legitimate risks and support them in this are likely to feel stressed and vulnerable in relation to the rest of the organisation, as their position denies them support from within the hierarchy. This is not to say that such conflicts should be avoided, but that managers have to be aware of them and find ways of getting support.

'Some level of cultural continuity is essential for maintaining co-operative relations, effective leadership styles and, above all, a sense of order that enables managers to make changes in some aspects of their work life' (Feldman, 1986). Culture is the context in which we work, and develop, through challenge, action, new policies, team building and through the way we manage. We are part of our organisation's culture but also are able to affect changes in it.

References

Stevenson and Parsloe (1981). *Social Services Area Teams*, Allen & Unwin.

Handy, C.(1981). *Understanding Organisations*, Penguin.

Harrison R.(1975). Understanding your organisation's character. *The 1975 Handbook for Group Facilitators*.

Peters and Waterman (1982). *In Search of Excellence*, Harper & Row.

Marshall & Maclean (1985). Exploring organisation culture as a route to organisational change. In *Current Research in Management*, Hammond, V., ed. F.Pinter.

Rothwell S.(1985). Is management a masculine role? *Management Education and Development*. Summer edn.

Davies J.(1985). Why are women not where the power is? *Management Education and Development*, Autumn edn.

Stewart R.(1976). *Contrasts in Management*, McGraw Hill.

Feldman S.(1986). Management in context: an essay on the relevance of culture to the understanding of organisational change. *Journal of Management Studies*, **23(6)**.

8 Working with outside projects

One of the consequences of the development of a mixed economy of welfare is that social services departments are no longer primarily the monopolistic providers of service. Instead, they will have to develop a more enabling, promotional and regulatory role. The effective implementation of the NHS and Community Care Act will mean that social services departments will need to involve voluntary organisations in strategic planning. Together, the voluntary and statutory sectors will need to develop a shared identification of need. Each will have significant contributions to make to producing Community Care plans and to communicating these to local communities. The capacity of the voluntary sector to hear the views of the user and potential users typically has been greater than that of government agencies. Appropriate community care will mean the skills of the voluntary sector will be more necessary than ever before. For the relationship to be optimised between statutory and voluntary sectors at local level, it will require the first-level managers to be tuned in as mediators and triggers to relevant and appropriate service developments and opportunities. Involvement in projects where they have none or limited direct control will become a more significant part of a manager's responsibilities. In a similar way to that operated in the social services departments, as the choice for users is extended, national voluntary organisations may set up new initiatives in partnership with other voluntary organisations, or community level initiatives. All projects will need managing. All may make demands of the new manager.

There have been an increasing number of 'partnership' projects and schemes in the UK over the last 15 years. The models include:

- Completely voluntary agency-run projects which seek local

authority, urban aid and central government money. They may also apply for funds from trusts such as Rainer, Rowntree, Leverhulme and the King's Fund. Save the Children, NCH and Barnardos have all developed a number of such schemes. They are often described as innovatory and experimental projects, though much voluntary organisation work remains traditional, routine service delivery. Social services managers may have to:

— liaise and assess applications for funding
— supervise staff
— become members or advisors on management and advisory committees
— produce reports and assessments on the work of such projects
— monitor spending and accounts
— be part of formal registration and inspection procedures.

● There are mixed economy projects where there is a multidisciplinary approach and multifunding. These may require funds from three local authority committees, eg for an Unemployed Workers' Centre, funding came from the community education, social work and employment committees, and some money from the women's committee. Funds were also obtained from central government grants and voluntary fund raising. The management issues in such projects, centre on whether the officials from the different departments can work together, as well as with local people and voluntary agency staff. Befriending is another area where social services departments have acted as part-funders and managers for the development of schemes. 'Cambridge Alternatives' is one of the best known and was directly supported by the social services department. Other initiators of such projects are Council of Voluntary Service (CVS) and national voluntary agencies.

● A third model involves the social services department in a form of radical community development. They are proactive in establishing a voluntary project. It can receive funds from the authority (and possibly others) to implement what is regarded strategically as an important piece of work but one where the authority does not carry the expertise. This has been the case in work in particularly deprived and vandalised estates, eg in work with the homeless (Shelter's involvement with Stopover hostels); work with housing associations for groups such as single, battered women and ethnic groups;

specialist work with offenders such as the establishment of motor and motorbike projects with young offenders (East Belfast and RUTS in Edinburgh). Research on schemes was undertaken by Vickery and Crosbie (unpublished observations) and is a useful reference document for those considering such projects.

Managing projects provides the opportunity for staff to become involved in pioneering and innovative work. However, the new manager needs to be aware of the many pitfalls and dangers in such projects, some of which are described below.

A community social work approach to practice, which Griffiths endorsed and offered the framework to achieve, has much in common with the requirements of working with these independent or partnership projects. Both share an emphasis on interagency work, innovation, and partnership with service users and local people.

His report showed that the development of community social work reflected the view of grass-roots workers that bureaucratically and centrally planned services did not meet the needs of individual communities or neighbourhoods. These community-focused workers were generally more aware and sensitive to local needs than were centrally based planners. This resulted from well-developed links with other agencies, community groups and local people. Together, they were in a position to identify the services which were really needed. Unfortunately, there was no mechanism for their views to be taken into account by the central planners.

Interagency local initiatives

To illustrate, young people were seen as a threat on an estate where there were few relevant resources for young people. This was evidenced by large numbers of young people grouping together in shopping areas particularly in the evening. The threat was more real than imagined to people going about their normal activities. The well-established co-operation between social workers, probation officers, community policemen and local churches provided an ideal forum for considering ways of helping relieve the situation. The result was a joint approach to several sources of funding, including small charitable organisations, in order to provide a detached youth work presence on the estate. This was seen as a more flexible response than the traditional ways of providing youth services. The worker was eventually placed in the probation office but accessible for all local agencies and interested community groups.

In time, the worker identified the lack of suitable accommodation as a major need of young people in the area. This was not only in the form of bedsits or flats but, more creatively, through the provision of a 'crash pad' where young people had the opportunity for periods of temporary respite from tensions at home. Over time, the worker and advisory committee were able to join with a housing association and voluntary trust to provide such a resource. It is unlikely that this would have been the outcome of the formal planning processes undertaken by senior staff in the respective organisations.

Effective local interagency co-operation takes time to develop and is a result of mutual trust and understanding. Sometimes, the manager's allegiance to such groups becomes greater than that to his/her own organisation. Such relationships appear to 'work' in that they provide responsive services to the expressed needs of the community. Equally significant is that they seem to provide considerable satisfaction for those involved. This is one reason why this is a beneficial way of developing new services.

In attempting to develop new services in this open and collaborative way, the process can be as rewarding and important as the outcome. A local group of workers, who provided services for pre-school children, agreed that a community resource centre for parents with young children would be of great benefit to the families in the area, and would also help their work. They wrote a joint letter to national and local child-care agencies asking for their help (and money) in establishing such a resource. It soon became clear that establishing a centre would not be possible. The effect, though, was to develop the working relationships of the group members. It helped those involved gain an understanding of the different responses that were possible. One way in which this was achieved was that some senior staff of Social Services came to talk with the group, because they were interested in the group's ideas. In doing so, they introduced some new perspectives and ideas from their own work. This was rewarding for the local group as it confirmed the value of their plans, and also provided some valuable contacts which were eventually used in different ways, one of which was as a training resource.

Manager's role

Involvement in projects provides a good way for new managers to develop skills such as negotiation and planning. New managers need to discuss their work with their own line managers. This will be necessary well before any definite commitment can be made on behalf of their departments. The first port of call may be someone who would be sympathetic to the ideas, rather than someone who would be threatened by them. This would not necessarily be the line manager, although the line manager would eventually need to know what was

happening. Line managers who are not kept involved and encouraged
to feel some ownership of a project can become obstructive. In
ignorance they can introduce an alien set of principles or issues, and
be unaware of the effect. The manager responsible may feel that the
line manager's views cannot be ignored but will be aware of the
potential damage. Diplomacy and educational skills will be required
here. An important skill is knowing the right people to talk to, at the
right time.

The skills and techniques for managing projects, where role and
control may be marginal, are substantially the same as those necessary
when the activity falls within the direct control and sole responsibility
of the manager's own organisation. Good managers should be able to
operate in both arenas. They need to be clear about the aims and
objectives of the work, and ensure there is general understanding and
acceptance of them, together with continuing to evaluate the work.

Management committees

A management committee may form the nerve centre for medium-to-
long-term strategy. The extent of involvement of the management
committee will depend on the persons involved, the nature of the
project and the strength/existence of day-to-day management. In
some instances extent of involvement could be marginal.

When a joint project is established, the input from the SSD or
national voluntary body may be a constitutional right to a substantial
number of voting places on the committee or secondment of a worker
who remains accountable to their agency.

In contrast, the SSD or national voluntary body may be a part, or
whole, funder but only hold advisory or observer seats on the
management committee. The created organisation is thus clearly
voluntary and independent.

It is more likely in the former case that the new manager may be
concerned with exercising a managerial role, though the financial
relationship and advisory role may mean that management skills are
drawn upon.

It is important for new managers to be aware of the limits of their
authority when speaking on behalf of their employing organisation.
Leaders of independently managed projects need to be aware of the
limits and extent of the authority of the agency representatives with
whom they are dealing. This is particularly important in respect of
their ability to commit finance. In addition, each member of any
management committee needs to be aware not only of their personal
authority, and the mandate with which they attend, but also that of
their co-members.

Management committees need to meet on a regular and understood cycle. Such meetings need to be recorded, and minutes circulated, so that everybody has the same understanding of what was agreed, and who is required to take action.

Conflicting values

Some of the local groups or community agencies with whom the manager will be working on the project may already be sophisticated with a strong identity. They may be organised as co-operatives, collectives or have some form of non-hierarchical user democracy at their heart. In any of these cases, a local authority manager, in particular, but also a manager from a large voluntary organisation may find him/herself in a clash of role perspectives and values. Sensitivity, awareness and flexibility will be essential if the manager is to get through this potential minefield.

It should not be assumed that the various agencies working together on a particular project will have the same values. Some preparatory work is required in order that values are made explicit both in terms of practice and management. This is likely to be most sensitive when the project is the result of a joint grass-roots initiative rather than one whose genesis arises from managers who have an explicit responsibility to understand and express the organisation's values. Expression does not necessarily mean that agreement will result. In some circumstances, the best that may be achieved is a coalition of conflicting or contrasting values.

For example, a voluntary agency may establish a family centre, based on community development principles, in an area where the local authority already has a family centre, based on therapeutic principles, working with families where children are at risk of abuse. Both enterprises are entirely legitimate but they have different roles and emphases. These need to be understood from the outset, otherwise confusion and difficulty will occur. Social workers may assume that the voluntary agency is an appropriate venue for access, rehabilitation or assessment visits for children in care. Such a use could be totally inappropriate, out of keeping with the aims and philosophies of the new centre, and could damage relationships.

In a situation such as this some ground rules are helpful. The local authority's role in child protection, for example, needs to be clearly understood by all involved, and a form of protocol agreed. It is too late to begin a discussion about what action is appropriate *after* the staff of a local project become aware of a family where children may be being abused. What to do in such a situation needs to be shared beforehand with agreement about what action is necessary and who are the right people to talk to. Such an understanding needs to extend beyond the managers directly involved to include other staff and local users. Similarly, how and whom the therapeutic family centre might direct to the community-orientated family centre needs clarifying. Involvement in one may not exclude involvement in the other.

Lack of management

Perhaps the biggest danger of a jointly managed project is that the managers are not, in fact, managed at all. They are allowed to drift. Those involved fail to agree a system of accountability or to define their respective roles. Management is seen usually as occurring within the 'home' organisation rather than within the project in question. In order to avoid this split, it is helpful to have a clear and agreed constitution, terms of reference or a written agreement and it may be necessary for this to have some form of legal base. There are recognised constitutions or memoranda of agreement which are easily applied to such situations.

These suggestions do not propose the imposition of an extensive bureaucracy but just tools which enable a project to work effectively.

Evaluation

Projects are no different from any other activity in that systems of evaluation are necessary. How this is to be done, by whom, and at what frequency, needs to be agreed at the outset. Users and volunteers need to be involved in defining performance indicators, deciding how the evaluation will be done, and by whom, and, where appropriate, doing some themselves. Evidence of effectiveness is crucial when funding is under threat or due for renewal. An evaluation report is much more valuable if it can demonstrate how the project has developed. An evaluation can also provide evidence of the standard of management. Evaluation should also lessen the chances of an inappropriate or duplicate service being provided through ignorance. Evaluation and monitoring are discussed in more detail in Chapter 11.

Innovation

The history of the voluntary sector is one of developing innovations for which the statutory sector eventually assumes responsibility. As the local authority's role in the provision of services declines, this is unlikely to be as common. The innovatory role should continue, as this is a good way for new developments to take place. Voluntary agencies need to remain interested in innovation. They are better able to take risks, unencumbered by the procedures and regulations referred to in Chapter 6. They are therefore prepared to invest in pioneering local projects.

Finance and staffing issues

A preoccupation for people involved with projects can be issues of finance. Managers should have an awareness of the various dimensions of finance. The voluntary sector relies significantly on financial contributions and referrals for service from local authorities. This is an integral part of the partnership. Very few projects are funded entirely through voluntary donations.

Projects are a good way of attracting 'opportunity money' such as through the Urban Programme. The criteria for this money generally includes innovatory services and this can be a good, quick way of getting things off the ground. Such schemes generally require a division in funding. For example, the Urban Programme provides 75% with the remaining 25% coming from the local authority, or from other sources. One way of doing this is for the voluntary agency to provide the 25% which means that hard-pressed local authorities make no financial contribution. It is useful to learn your way around this maze, or to make an alliance with someone who does. It is time well spent and can be the key to obtaining the all too necessary funding.

Under the NHS and Community Care Act there are further inducements to local authorities to withdraw from led control and to develop mixed funding packages when purchasing care. Purchasing care may actually mean the development of a local scheme to serve several people with similar needs in one locality. Under the Act, social services departments have a responsibility to generate more not-for-profit/non-statutory providers of services.

One of the major drawbacks of project funding is that funds are generally on a time-limited basis laid out in a contract. This needs to be taken into account from the outset. Is it to be a short-term project or are there ways of securing long-term funding? This is particularly important if staff are to be employed in the project. A danger is that the maintaining of funding becomes the preoccupation of managers. The main activities of the project can get inadequate attention. This can breed insecurity which is totally disabling.

If staff leave during a fixed-term project which will not receive further monies, maintaining momentum and achieving project objectives can be particularly problematic. Understandably, some staff will leave to protect their own continuity of employment. This needs to be discussed between staff and responsible manager.

Together, they may be able to devise proposals for new projects that the workers can move on to. They could actively plan for users to take over the project during its lifetime with the worker increasingly taking a 'back seat'. In this way, leaving will not traumatise the project.

It may be some comfort that, in many ways, local authority culture has become similar to that of the voluntary sector. There is now less guarantee of long-term security. Re-organisations, service changes and cutbacks are a fact of life. It is part of the manager's task not only to cope with the personal effects of this but also to explain to staff that insecurity is now the norm. It can be reframed as 'change' which can encourage constant progression not stagnation. But it must be managed. It seems that many people now need to acknowledge that their working arrangements may well change at least every two to three years. This can be planned for, and be seen as positive.

A further complexity in respect of funding projects can be the budget process. Participating organisations have different timescales for budget development. This can be hard to co-ordinate, as funding from one source can be dependent on that from another, yet agreement may not come simultaneously. For a project which relies on funding from various sources, the decision of one agency to reduce or stop this can place the whole enterprise in jeopardy. This is particularly true in times of reducing public expenditure when an early response to this pressure can be to reduce grants to the voluntary agencies. Although understandable, in the sense that a social services department or national voluntary organisation's first priority is generally its own staff, the result can be very frustrating and require tremendous efforts in order to preserve the future of the project. This is particularly so where it is known to provide a valued and important local service.

Political dimensions

The scale of projects varies. There may be the large authority or area-wide projects perhaps involving the social services and a major national agency, eg Children's Society, MIND or Age Concern, in partnership. Alternatively, there may be the small locality-based projects which can also involve such agencies or local groups. A common feature of such enterprises is that they are a crucial part of the political power base of local councillors or other significant community activists.

Managers involved in this work should try to become as aware as possible of the different agendas of those involved. Local politicians can have real influence in management committees and can use them as an arena for other battles totally unconnected with the enterprise in hand.

Political activists or community leaders can also use projects as a power base. Their purpose in doing so may be unconnected with the goals of the organisation. For example, one constitution of some projects invites both group and individual membership. This can be used as a mechanism for interested parties to gain control of the significant resources involved. New managers need to be aware of this, and act if faced with such an eventuality.

Equal opportunities

As in all organisations, many significant decisions may be taken by subgroups away from the formal arena. The appointment of staff, for example, can be used to place allies in positions of influence or as a reward for services rendered. It is not unusual for a project to be set up only to find that the posts available are filled in this way. This may mean that it is the best people who get the jobs, but the unsuspecting and innocent manager would rightly be concerned. To build in equal opportunities practices for projects at the outset may be an initiative the manager has to take. It will not just happen. Where there is multiple management and joint funding, difficulties may arise over employment issues such as grievances and disciplinary proceedings. This can be particularly acute when staff are seconded and have two 'masters'. These complex issues need active management that is visible to all those involved.

Local representation and involvement

It is usual for first-line managers to be asked to act as representatives on local bodies such as Councils for Voluntary Service. This can provide a useful introduction to work with the voluntary sector, can help to develop local contacts and raise awareness of the various political machinations that take place. It is also a good way of gaining entry to significant and powerful local networks. It is interesting to see how many of the same people turn up at meetings of all the various active organisations in an area.

As in all social work activities, managers should make every effort to listen to the views of, and work in partnership with, service users. This can neither be imposed nor does it develop overnight as it takes time for the necessary trust to be developed. Mechanisms are required continually to check out the views and needs of consumers in respect of proposed projects. It can be dangerous to make assumptions about the involvement and views of local people even in a well-established project.

A community development scheme, for example, jointly managed by the local authority and by the Children's Society was reviewed after eight years' successful operation. Throughout its life, the emphasis had been on involving local people and on providing services which were in line with their views of their needs. It was only during this review, when independent interviewers talked to people who used the centre, that it became glaringly apparent that they felt they had no voice in its management. One of the recommendations of the review was that the users of the centre should have an equal voice on the management committee.

This was agreed enthusiastically by the Society and by the local authority as being entirely consistent with the aims of the project. It formally recognised the contribution and importance of a resident's perspective and also gave local people an insight into the many difficulties there were in managing the project, eg monitoring the funding and caring for the building.

In spite of the enthusiasm and commitment of the managers from the agencies involved, it still took considerable time and negotiation for local people actively to take part on a management committee. This was in spite of the fact that everyone involved already knew one another. The professionals had to agree to make a conscious effort to speak in jargon-free language and to conduct the meetings in an informal manner that would be comfortable for the local representatives. Principles of rotating the chair and secretary for meetings had to balance everyone in the group being treated equally against not asking people to do things they were not comfortable with.

As a way of confirming where they stood, the local representatives asked the main grade project workers to make a video in which each member of the management group explained who they were, what their job was and what was their involvement with the project. The aim was to provide an insight into the world of the other members of the group so they would not be going into the first meeting 'cold'. This was followed by a number of informal 'get togethers' of the group prior to the first meeting under the new 'constitution'. This preparation appeared to be effective in developing a new approach to managing the project, more importantly it provided a salutary lesson for the professionals involved who already thought they had a partnership with the local community. It needed more than a mere invitation for them to be able to participate! The success of this can be judged by the fact that subsequently it was the user participants who gave the annual report to the council committee responsible for monitoring the local authority's financial contribution to the project.

Advocacy and campaigning

Such activities may not be common, but there are examples of organised groups attempting to take over legitimate and respected national charities in order to further their own ends.

Voluntary agencies can play the role of service provider or pressure group and often do both at the same time. Involvement with them can enable social services staff to put pressure on their own authority in a way which they are not usually in a position to do. One way is through the advocacy movement where people speak on behalf of individual service users. This simultaneously may allay the expression of the views of the staff themselves. Such pressure also provides a check on the power of local authorities. Voluntary groups are often better placed to put pressure on other local authority departments in a way that is not possible for lower level managers. For example, while social services departments will have formal liaison arrangements with housing departments, organisations such as Age Concern and the Children's Society are in a better position to gain publicity on behalf of their constituents against actions of local councils. Poll tax resistance has been one issue where managers and staff from social services departments have found themselves in breach of SSD/local authority policy, as projects have become the co-ordinating forces in opposing the community charge. Becoming involved in such activities can be dangerous and inappropriate. Social services managers have to make their formal position clear, and colleagues from the voluntary sector have to understand and respect this.

Managers as resources

Social work managers can bring particular skills or resources to local groups such as that of chairing and organising meetings or providing assistance with typing, copying or other clerical tasks. This can be especially useful in the early stages of a project's life. In addition they often are able to assist groups in finding their way through the local authority maze which can be very frustrating, time consuming and debilitating. The wider the range of contacts that managers develop, the greater will be their ability to point people in the right direction.

In offering these skills and resources, managers should try to recognise that their role is one of enabling rather than controlling. The culture may also be different from that of their usual workplace. For example, decisions may take longer and be via a more tortuous route, but this process is likely to be important for the project and the temptation to be autocratic in order to save time should be resisted.

Diplomatic skills, as ever, are important, as is recognising and valuing the contribution of everybody involved.

There will be times when involvement in this work can bring managers into conflict with their own agency. It is important constantly to reassess where loyalties lie. There will be times when it will be legitimate to take risks in supporting the needs of the project *vis-à-vis* the manager's own agency. A manager should pick the issues which s/he is confident of winning, and which are legitimate in terms of fitting in with the agency's long-term objectives. There is a danger for the local authority manager of becoming over-identified in supporting the voluntary sector. It can result in a reputation of 'maverick', someone seen as more suited to working outside the agency. This is a matter of judgement and depends on an assessment of the manager's long-term future. A helpful benchmark may be to check to what extent the action taken is attempting to achieve the service goals of your department.

In spite of the dangers and pitfalls of becoming involved in projects, some of which are identified above, it can be a very rewarding and important experience for managers. Involvement in projects provides the opportunity to:

- develop and support new and innovative services
- acquire a broad range of managerial and political skills
- work alongside users and other local people in running and managing projects
- develop interagency relationships and the positive use of volunteers which can be beneficial in other situations. It is a way of working demanded by both the Children Act 1989 and the NHS Community Care Act 1990
- more directly meet the needs of users
- encourage recalcitrant agencies and authorities to work co-operatively
- respond flexibly to changing conditions
- take risks by not being tied to the 'rules' of Social 'Services'
- use contracts as a tool to ensure that the integrity and wishes of users are fully taken into account.

The manager does not necessarily go into projects either as leader or expert, but may be expected to use elements of leadership and expertise by virtue of position and background. The more respect the manager shows for the experience and knowledge held by users, other agencies and by local people, the greater chance of mutual co-operation and of a successful project.

As in other managerial activities, it is people with the energy and the will to succeed who will be able to make a success of these projects.

If they are worthwhile and ultimately provide a better service for people, then the risks involved are worth taking. If the reverse is true, then it is better to withdraw and devote your energies to other issues.

Nevertheless try to become involved with some projects as the skills and experience which you will develop will not only have service implications but also can play a significant factor in your own personal development, and provide satisfaction (and frustration) in your working life.

Reference
Crosbie, D. and Vickery, A. (1989), Community Based Schemes in Area Offices. Report to DoH. Spring Unpublished.

Part 3
Some management tools

9 Budgeting

Introduction

Just as someone once said that *Watership Down* told her more about rabbits than she needed to know, this chapter includes a comprehensive analysis of budgeting, not all of which will be immediately relevant to team leaders.

It is included, however, in order to provide the complete map within which you may find it helpful to select some details for special study that will help you to place things in perspective. Above all, we hope it will give you confidence to approach the new era of budgeting, aware of the opportunities as well as of the complexities.

Social services agencies are moving rapidly into an era when team managers will be required to be able to handle a wider range of financial processes than at present. This requirement will apply to those whose roles are broadly case management, and to those who are involved in service delivery.

Responsibilities are increasingly likely to include making a contribution to formulating the annual budget of the agency as a whole, and carrying out routine monitoring and evaluation of current expenditure.

Team managers, as well as taking on this role themselves, will be able to involve the members of their teams at different stages, as appropriate.

In addition, their new financial powers may allow them to be more creative in the scope of their community social work. For example, there may be opportunities to help new organisations to enter the world of service delivery. A team manager may be able to provide some of the financial and other advice which will allow a community group to compete successfully against existing suppliers for a contract.

Why do we produce budgets?

There are many reasons for producing budgets. Principally, making a budget helps to plan and co-ordinate the coming year's activities. It also communicates plans to managers and motivates them to strive to achieve the organisational goals. Budgeting also puts a control on activities and evaluates the way in which managers perform.

Planning

The budgeting process should be relevant and should include the participation of managers throughout the organisation. Without the budgeting process, the pressures of day-to-day operating problems can easily tempt managers not to plan their future operations. Involving them in budgeting ensures that managers do plan, consider how conditions in the next year might change and decide on what steps they should take to respond. Equally, they may have identified conditions they wish to change and can accommodate this process within the budgeting framework. The process encourages managers to anticipate problems before they arise and minimise the number of hasty decisions.

Co-ordination

The budget is a vehicle through which the actions of the different parts of the organisation can be brought together into a common plan. Without co-ordination, each manager makes their own plans unchecked, believing that they are working in the best interests of the customer and the organisation. The budgeting process needs, therefore, to be structured in a way which compels managers to examine the relationship between their own operations and interests, the needs and resources in their areas, with those of other departments or other sections involved in the process. It is unlikely that first drafts will represent a meshing of the organisational activities, but a sound budgeting system will co-ordinate these separate activities and gradually aggregate, and rationalise them into a sensible whole.

Communication

In order to function effectively, an organisation must have clearly understood lines of communication which ensure all parts are fully informed of the plans, policies and the constraints to which the organisation is expected to conform. Everyone in the organisation should have a clear understanding of the part they are expected to play in achieving the annual budget. The process will ensure that the appropriate individuals are made accountable for implementing the budget. These are likely to be middle managers or perhaps the newly termed 'care managers'. They take responsibility for communicating the purpose and process of budgeting to their staff. As the knowledge of needs and resources and plans made at local level are communicated and aggregated throughout the department, top managers have a responsibility to ensure that what cascades back down in a final form is understood by everyone. The exchange of information is vital.

Motivation

The budget can be a useful device in influencing and motivating managers. However, it is equally true that budgets can act as an encouragement to inefficiency and conflict between managers. For instance, if the budget is dictated from above, and imposes a threat rather than a challenge, it may be resisted and do more harm than good. In one authority, the central finance section allocated money without negotiation and a printing budget was allocated assuming that the need in four divisions was the same. In practice, the need differed greatly, and the allocation led to in-fighting.

Control

A budget can assist managers in managing and controlling the activities for which they are responsible. By comparing the actual results with the budgeted amounts for different categories of expenditure, managers can ascertain which costs do not conform to the original plan. By concentrating on significant deviations, they will be able to identify any inefficiencies that may have occurred. This may be the lack of uptake of bed space in a residential establishment, or a failure to use an agreed amount of money for community project activities. The manager may be able to assist!

Performance evaluation

In some organisations, a manager's performance can be evaluated by measuring success in meeting budget targets. But, if this is overemphasised in non-profit making organisations, such an expectation can distort the more creative and flexible function that budgets should have in matching needs to resources. Success in meeting a target could then be narrowly measured by noting the full expenditure of the budget for children in care, for instance, and evaluation would fail to identify that an underspend results from successful rehabilitation work.

The budget period

A detailed budget for each responsibility centre, that is devolved budgets, could place the budget allocation at the team manager level. Such budgets normally are prepared for one year. The annual budget may be divided either into 12 monthly or 13 four-weekly periods. As the year goes by, the period for which a budget is available will shorten until the budget for the next year is prepared. So, management and planning are not connected consistently to a firm knowledge of the long-term financial plan.

Alternatively, the annual budget may be broken down by months for the first three months, by quarters for the remaining nine months. On a rolling programme, the quarterly budgets are developed, month on month, as the year proceeds. For example, during the first quarter, the monthly budgets for the second quarter will be prepared, and during the second quarter the monthly budgets for the third quarter will be prepared. This makes review an in-built part of the budget cycle, if adequate time is available. For example, during the first quarter, the budget for the next three quarters may be changed as new information has become available. A new budget for a fifth quarter will also be prepared. This process is known as continuous, or 'rolling budgeting', and ensures that a 12-month budget is always available by adding a quarter in the future as the quarter just ended is dropped. Rolling budgets ensure that planning is not something which takes place once a year when the budget is being formulated.

Rolling budgeting is a continuous process and managers are encouraged constantly to look ahead and review their future plans. It is likely that actual performance will be compared with a more realistic target because budgets are being constantly reviewed and updated. There is a danger, though, that the fear of constant revisions may lead budget staff to fail to give sufficient attention to preparing the new budget for the next quarter.

Irrespective of which system is used, it is important that four-weekly budgets are used for control purposes. Without such management, it is likely that 'shock' overspends or underspends will occur when the new budget is being planned, and will distort the planning and targeting for subsequent years.

Initial preparation and negotiation of budgets

Managers who are responsible for meeting the budgeted performance should prepare the budget for their own areas. The preparation of the budget should be a bottom-up process — the bidet effect. The budget should originate at the lowest levels of management, and be refined and co-ordinated at higher levels. This will allow managers to participate, and increases the probability that they will accept the budget, and will strive to achieve the targets.

The principle is one of a pyramid. Managers at the lowest level, having assessed the needs and resources required to achieve their targets at local level, submit these in budgetary terms to their superiors for approval. The superior then incorporates the one budget with the others for the area, and then submits this aggregated budget for approval to their superior, who then becomes the budgetee at the next level (Fig. 9.1).

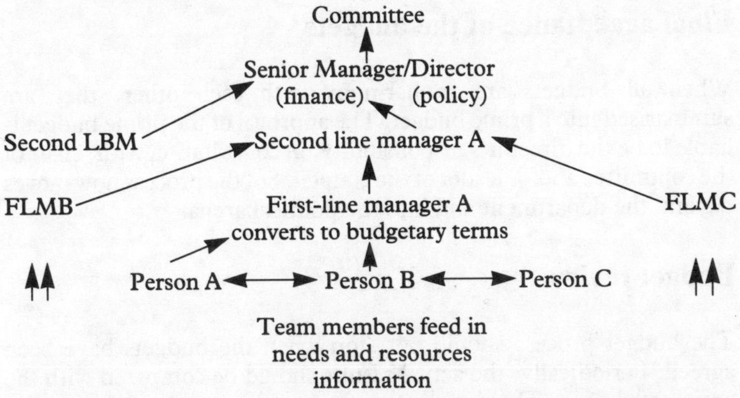

Fig. 9.1 Pictorial representation of the aggregation of information up the organisation. The framework may have been determined by treasurer's or social work committee.((F) LMB = (First) - line manager B).

It is important for the supervisor of this process to be clear that the subordinate can justify the needs behind his, or her, budget plans. In the initial phases of participation, first-line managers' limited experience may lead them to make inadequate requests. It is quite appropriate for different levels of expenditures to enter into the budget at different levels within the organisation (see below).

The negotiating process is of vital importance in budgeting and can determine whether the budget becomes a really effective management tool or just a set of inert data. If managers are successful in establishing a position of trust and confidence with their

subordinates, the negotiation process will produce a meaningful
improvement in the budgetary process.

Co-ordination and review of budgets

As the individual budgets move up the organisational hierarchy in the
negotiation process, they must be examined in relation to each other.
This examination may indicate that some budgets are out of balance
with others and need modifying so that they will be compatible with
the other conditions, constraints and plans which are beyond that
particular manager's knowledge or control. Any changes in the
budget should be made by the responsible managers, and may require
that the budgets be recycled from the bottom to the top for a second,
or even for a third time, until all the budgets are co-ordinated and
acceptable to all the parties involved.

Final acceptance of the budgets

When all budgets are in harmony with each other, they are
summarised into a prime budget. The approval of the prime budget is
liable to be the director's responsibility, in consultation with, chair of
the committee and/or leader of the council. So, the process now moves
beyond the department and into the political arena.

Budget review

The budget process should not stop when the budgets have been
agreed. Periodically, the actual results should be compared with the
anticipated ones. These comparisons should be made on a monthly
basis and a report sent to the appropriate budgetees before the middle
of the following month so that it has the maximum motivational
impact. This will enable management to identify the items which are
not proceeding according to plan, and to investigate the reasons for
the difference.

If these differences are within management control, corrective
action can be taken to avoid similar inefficiencies recurring. But the
differences could be due to an unrealistic budget or to a change in
conditions. Without adjustments, the budget for the remainder of the
year would be invalid with potentially disastrous results. It is
important to emphasise that the budgetary process does not stop at the
end of a year. Budgeting should be seen as a continuous and a dynamic
process.

In one authority the research and development unit provides all team managers with an open learning course to ensure they are fully finance and computer literate.

Computerised budgeting

In today's world, budgeting is usually computerised. The organisation could choose a computer program written specifically, an accounting package or a commercial spreadsheet such as Lotus 123, or VP Planner. These are available from most software houses. Instead of the accounting staff being primarily concerned with numerical manipulation, they can, with a computer's help, become part of the real planning process. They can advise managers by getting information and presenting it in a way that is relevant to the budgeting process.

With a personal computer, managers can look at several different options before agreeing a budget. Even when it has been agreed, the budget can be quickly revised without a great deal of effort. So, it is possible to take risks, to ask 'what if,' and to foresee the outcomes.

The budgeting process

The budgeting process normally begins when managers calculate the costs of maintaining and developing activities. Accountants then produce an overall budget proposal. Available resources for the proposed expenditure level should be sufficient to cover the total costs of providing the services. A local authority raises the financial resources, from poll tax and government grants. In future, local authorities may be able to obtain other forms of income by negotiating with private companies. (This would previously have been limited to urban aid grants and to other forms of grant aiding, liable to come from central government sources only.)

There should also be an opportunity for local teams and work units to be more imaginative and creative in securing funding, like asking a local firm with a predominantly female workforce to finance a crèche. But, while a local team may be able to initiate the idea, the final decision will probably take place at the most senior level of the organisation. So, the more viable the plan, the more chance of success it will have. Directors and senior managers may see local teams as proactive and innovative. Such a shift in culture could also bring shared responsibility to provide services, both throughout the organisation and between the local authority and the profit-making organisations in the locality.

Valuing outputs

The difficulty is that outputs in social services cannot be measured readily in monetary terms. (By outputs we mean the quality and amount of the services that are rendered.) In profit-orientated organisations, output can be measured in terms of sales revenue. The effect of this is that budgets in 'non-profit' organisations tend to be concerned mainly with expenditure and not income beyond that raised at the outset through the poll tax and government grants.

In social services, there is perhaps insufficient emphasis on the objectives of resourcing. The budgeting process tends to link what is happening with the cash available. There is very little emphasis on measuring managerial performance at middle manager level. Equally, there is very little assessment of what the practitioner achieves in terms of time, skills and resources. This is because there is no clear relationship between the resources applied to a particular need and the benefits which flow from the use of those resources. However, increasing efforts are being made to overcome these deficiencies by developing measures of outputs which can be used to compare budgeted and actual accomplishments within a professional context.

Budgets explained

The word budget commonly means the allocation of an overall sum of money to a manager to control. The notion of a lump sum conjures up a picture of freedom to spend on any mixture of staffing, supplies, equipment and so on that would best attain the local objectives. This type of budget, often referred to as a *bottom-line budget* is seen by some as the most desirable form of budget to be placed with first-line managers, and by others as a ridiculous devolution of power. Whichever view is taken of its desirability, it is a medium–to long-term goal, not one to be aimed for at the outset of devolving budgets as is indicated in 'Caring for People'.

The reasons for taking an incremental approach to the ultimate freeing up of budgets include:

- the need to constrain managerial spending in the early years of devolution until all have developed the confidence that first-line managers can control their own budgets
- corporate control of staffing. This is often used by elected members as the ultimate lever to pull if the authorities forecast expenditure is overshooting its budget, or if a cut in overall budget is forced on the local authority from outside. A good deal of negotiation is needed to begin to make flexible

budgets. Flexibility would mean that money allocated to wages can be switched to salaries and vice versa, and to and from both these budget headings to other expenditures, for example, to supplies and equipment.

Line budgets specify the amount of money that can be spent on different items, for example, on basic salaries, overtime, provisions, cleaning materials, and can occur at any level in the department, usually determined by the view of politicians, treasurers and senior social work staff. Each of the items is listed on a separate line of the budget with the budgeted amount alongside, hence the term 'line budget' (Table 9.1).

Table 9.1 Extract from a line budget

Item	Budget (£s)
Salaries— basic	100 000
Salaries — overtime	10 000
Wages — basic	75 000
Wages — overtime	5 000
Provisions	40 000
Equipment	12 000
Utilities bills	3 000

The problem with devolving budgets in this form arises from inflexible rules which govern the degree to which the budget on one line can be drawn upon to supplement that of another line. There are two ways in which this switching of expenditure can occur. Part of the budget can be moved from one line to another. This switching of budgets is referred to as *virement*. Once the budget has been switched, expenditure can then continue to be incurred up to the new budget limit. Alternatively, an overspend on one line of the budget can be agreed as long as it is matched by a corresponding underspend on another.

Where switching of expenditure takes place formally, it is subject to a set of formal rules sometimes referred to as *standing orders* or *financial regulations*. These are the rules for regulating the way in which budgets may be used within any section of the local authority. Generally, they place a limit on how much may be vired from one budget head to another (eg £5000) and whose permission must be sought either in the finance department, or at committee level if this limit is to be exceeded.

One of the early steps that is being taken towards developed resource management is to reduce the restrictions on shifting

expenditure between budget lines. Some authorities have raised the
virement limits considerably, others have made unlimited virement
possible within certain groups of budget lines. These budget lines
tend not to be those concerned with wages and salaries.

Management accounts

Line budgets provide information on the inputs, eg labour and
materials that the manager is using to ensure services are delivered.
Hence, monitoring expenditure against budget shows which inputs
contain slack or an actual or projected overspend. This is useful as far
as it goes, but managers are concerned with why they are over—or
underspent rather than the mere fact they are. Is it to do with an
increase in the number of clients being served or to do with more
clients requiring a more intensive service with different working
practices? The line budget format is unable to meet these information
needs. Financial information needs to be supplemented by
information on clients and services. This transforms the budget from
being a *financial account* to a *management account*.

Management accounts record expenditure by inputs and some
other factor. Typically, in social services, this would be by type of
service, or client group, or both. Hence the line budget in Table 9.1
would be recast as follows for a service budget and for a client budget.

Table 9.2 A service budget

Service A (day centre)	
Salaries — basic	20 000
Salaries — overtime	2 000
Wages — basic	5 000
Wages — overtime	1 000
Provisions	2 000
Equipment	1 000
Utilities bills	500
Service B (homecare)	
Salaries — basic	80 000
Salaries — overtime	8 000
Wages — basic	70 000
Wages — overtime	4 000
Provisions	38 000
Equipment	11 000
Utilities bills	2 500

Table 9.3 A client group budget

Client group 1 (elderly people)

Salaries — basic	65 000
Salaries — overtime	6 500
Wages — basic	72 000
Wages — overtime	3 000
Provisions	29 000
Equipment	9 800
Utilities bills	2 300

Client group 2 (mentally ill people)

Salaries — basic	35 000
Salaries — overtime	3 500
Wages — basic	23 000
Wages — overtime	1 900
Provisions	10 800
Equipment	2 200
Utilities bills	700

Table 9.4 A joint client group and service budget

Client group 1 (Elderly people)	Service A (day centre)	Service B (home care)
Salaries — basic	15 000	50 000
Salaries — overtime	2 500	5 000
Wages — basic	2 000	50 000
Wages — overtime	100	3 000
Subtotal	19 600	108 000
Provisions	1 200	28 000
Equipment	800	9 000
Utilities bills	300	2 000
Subtotal	2 300	54 000
Total	21 000	147 000

Table 9.4 continued

Client group 2 (mentally ill people)

Salaries — basic	5 000		30 000
Salaries — overtime	500		3 000
Wages — basic	3 000		20 000
Wages — overtime	900		1 000
Subtotal	9 400	54 000	
Provisions	800		10 000
Equipment	200		2 000
Utilities bills	200		500
Subtotal	1 200	12 500	
Total	10 600		66 500

These examples of management accounts begin to allow managers to ask more pointed questions. For example, why is the cost of salaries higher for service B (homecare) to client group 1 (elderly people) than for client group 2 (mentally ill people). A number of explanations are possible. More clients of group 1 may be served, or clients may be provided with a more intensive service, or require more highly skilled workers who command higher salaries. Although the management accounts point towards such explanations, they do not provide the kind of information needed to decide which explanation is right. This can be achieved by supplementing the financial information with further information; on the services provided, staffing levels and the number of clients served. These can be combined with one another to form *performance indicators*.

Performance indicators

Table 9.5 illustrates how the budget material from the client and service management accounts can be combined with a few basic staff, client and service statistics to begin to reveal the reasons behind the differing costs of the services to the two client groups.

Table 9.5 Performance information examples

	Client group 1 (elderly people)		Client group 2 (mentally ill people)	
	Service A (day centre)	Service B (homecare)	Service A (day centre)	Service B (homecare)
Total number of clients served	200	500	50	85
Total number of service sessions	5200	4850	7500	3500
Average number of sessions per client	1 per week	1 per week	5 per week	7 per week
Number of salaried staff	5	2	2	2
Total number of clients per salaried member of staff	40	250	25	44
Number of waged staff	4	25	8	10
Total number of clients per waged member of staff	50	20	6.2	8.5
Total cost per client served	£109.50	£294.00	£210.20	£780.00
Total client sessions per salaried member of staff			and so on	
Total client sessions per waged member of staff				
Total cost per client session				
Total salaried staff cost per client served				
Total wages cost per client served.				

Table 9.5 makes it possible to spot which of the services has the most clients, and which provides the most intensive service per client (service sessions per client). If neither client volume or service intensity sufficiently explains the budget differences, then the staffing costs are investigated (staff per client served). This can be broken

down further to take into account the differing intensities of service.

Whether budgets are devolved, and, if so, to what level, along with the separation of client and service budgets, are decisions made by individual authorities at committee level. They thus vary in practice across the UK.

Common features in the local authority budget process

1. In June, July and August, senior elected members guide the director of the relevant department on changes likely to be possible in the next budget. This is a point of initial influence.
2. Treasurers issue planning ground rules, a mixture of base updates and likely grant positions.
3. There is normally a high-level political process amongst chair people of service committees which agree overall spending priorities.
4. Committee briefings are issued. They spell out the financial implications of major issues facing departments.
5. Committees are given guidelines by the leader, which set the overall budget level. If this is not possible, because of political or grant uncertainty, alternative guidelines may be issued.
6. Committees refer to their own previously agreed priorities in order to arrive at their budget distribution.
7. Detailed budgets are given to the people responsible for spending them. This occurs relatively late on, if at all, and in some cases, after the beginning of the financial year.

This outlines the traditional, top-down budgeting process from which local teams and lower level managers are excluded. It is evident that at certain points (such as 6), priorities could, and should, have been influenced by the local team's view of necessary resources.

The notion of care managers and the principle underlying the Griffiths report imply further involvement of lower levels of management and local teams development. Staff who currently spend little time on planning will clearly need more space to do so. The planning process, which culminates in the final budget allocation, must be structured, must link in and across all levels in the organisation, and, most importantly, must be understood and communicable.

If staff do not feel committed to the budgets with which they are presented, it is likely that deviant behaviour will occur, such as deliberate overspending or miscoding.

The discussion of power in the operating units requires us to consider the implications of the social services becoming an agency which buys in services from state, and voluntary private service providers as the Government intends.

The enabling function of SSDs will require significant changes in attitude, practice and procedures in terms of the controls and mechanisms which currently exist within social services departments. If traditional budgeting models are maintained, it is likely they will break down and will need to be replaced by a budgeting process which is based on a model of participation and of a split between procurers and providers of services. Bottom-up budgeting, aggregated in the form discussed earlier in this chapter, should allow for wholesale switching of expenditures between staff and between budget heads. Guidance must be given to first-line managers on the minimum expected services. The minimum outcomes must be understood and may act as a measure of performance. The involvement of first-line managers and their teams raises the question of their negotiation and involvement at local level with elected members in assessing local needs and resources. Equally, as is highlighted in an example by Joyce Moseley in the Chapter 13, it is possible at local level for local people themselves to be involved in, and influence, the planning that will feed into the aggregated budgeting system. The implications of a participative system which has consumer influence must be that, if a team could buy a service from another source more cheaply than it can be provided by the agency itself, or with added beneficial effects, it should be free to do so. The pricing mechanism for central services needs to be, therefore, more flexible, more accurate and more relevant so that choices can be realistic. Such a change could be seen as very threatening to the corporate services within an authority.

While local teams once educated and trained in budgetary and financial perspectives value the participation and control they may have in the allocation of resources, they will also need to take on board that they should be held to account for errors and misappropriation within the budgetary system. It must be clear who, precisely, can be regarded as the budget holders, and for them to be in a responsible relationship to those people who may be influencing, advising and negotiating with the public, local members and the teams themselves on the level of need to be addressed and the required resources. It would be neither appropriate nor adequate for a resource to be requested by a local team and aggregated through the system if it was chosen on the personal/professional preference of the workers rather than deriving from a need that could be identified and clarified through both hard and soft data sources.

10 Creating an informative environment

Information

Information is a powerful tool which has traditionally been undervalued and underused. Acquiring information and managing it is complex and time consuming. Consumer-led rather than organisation-led decisions require the creation of participative and informative environments. This means reorganisations which take account of information presented by consumers as well as professionals, and create a means for their views and knowledge to become part of the system that informs decisions.

Centralising information is relevant only when it increases efficiency in a way that makes sense to the consumer. Managers can be mediators for the data coming into the organisation. It is also a management task to organise the data into information that is accessible and useful to both staff and consumers.

What is and what is not information?

It is all too easy to fall into the trap of accumulating data. Data in themselves are of limited value. They are meaningless as they have no foci. But, if they have been collected and framed for a specific use they become information and are usable. The transition from data to information involves a process: the data are sifted; gaps are acknowledged; further data are collected. What results has then to be presented in a way that makes sense to the recipient. For the consumer or other agency, it must be devoid of professional jargon.

For internal purposes, it should be succinct and explicitly linked to existing activity or discussions. If framed in a careful and well-thought out manner, the manager will be more effective in influencing both public partnership, practice and policy. Whilst this process may be methodical, valuable information may not always be generated from rational data — census statistics, for example. There must be an openness and a fusion of the rational and random. As the popular writer on management, Robert Waterman (1982), puts it 'We live in a probablistic and not a deterministic world'.

Data that are presented by an individual, team or local group are described as 'soft'. The 'hard' format of research and statistics, however, is often given greater credence than 'what the people say'. Qualitatively useful information should be a thorough and unprejudiced synthesis of both. This requires continual update, review and resynthesis if information is going to be dynamic and real for people. To achieve keeping data relevant will require the manager to develop good relationships with the team administrator, in particular, but with people in general in the locality.

Why information? — why be informed?

Widespread availability of information is the only basis for effective day-to-day problem-solving. 'An individual without information can not take responsibility; an individual who is given information cannot help but take responsibility' (Jan Carlzon RIV PYRAMIDERNA, (1987),). Placed in the context of such as the Children Act 1989 where an emphasis on shared responsibility permeates the legislation, the significance of information as a tool of empowerment is clear. It is thus essential that managers and their staff get to grips with managing information in a way that can be retained, and thus retain professional power. Sharing information inhibits power games and encourages effective participation.

Information gathering is time consuming but the process will give the gatherer a rich vision. If an off-site manager deals with his team on the telephone, there will be no real sense of the relationships between team members on a daily basis — until perhaps an explosion takes place!

Similarly, if a worker is asked to find out how many elderly people live in a road, it can either be done by statistical data, by door-knocking, or by asking people in the local launderette how many elderly people live in their road. In terms of useful data to make decisions the outcome of answers such as 'six people', from the hard data source, rather than 'six people, three of whom live with relatives, one is very ill and the other two are always out and do the bingo at the centre each week' from the soft data source bears no comparison.

A soft data method will take longer but will be qualitatively more valuable. The manager's task will be to push people to gather soft data with the administrator creating frameworks for storage and retrieval. The manager may need to be involved in the process of collection, both to model and endorse its value at the outset. There are times when hard data are appropriate. If the chief executive asked how many elderly people lived in a street for a committee item, due that night, on the relevance of street warden schemes, then pure statistics would be adequate. But, for the team which wishes to create a spirit of empowerment for those living in a locality, the appropriate action is to talk *to* local people, and not *about* them.

Information can make staff more productive

An increased understanding of the strengths in the communities served will ensure that the service delivered is more relevant. A team is able to consume more work when it feels in partnership with the people. Instead of a referral being seen as a problem for social services to solve alone, it can be seen as a means of contact and brokerage with, and between, local people.

One team who held a store of information on local people outside of case files was able to respond thus. An elderly couple needed support due to the husband suffering from Huntington's chorea. They were referred to social services. The staff knew the neighbourhood and the general facilities available there. By going out and talking with nearby neighbours, the social workers were able to set up a network of 24-hour local support supplemented by health care services. To make the judgement that local people would be prepared to co-operate, with the couple's permission, required knowledge of general attitudes, norms and the willingness of particular individuals who may have had contact with social services themselves.

The team held cards with a few lines of known examples of help people gave to each other, or of the key 'informants' or gatekeepers of what help may be available. It was important to ensure this data were not just held in the heads of experienced workers but were available to the whole team. As manager, and supervisor, the team leader is, in many cases, in a key position to remind staff to log such data and of the importance of team sharing.

It may be interesting to note that the team that worked in this way had an average staff turnover of five years when the professional norm at the time was two years. To be well informed reduces anxiety and broadens the options for action.

Information is essential for planning and strategy

Waterman (1982), is extremely critical of the old school 'traditional manager' who sees his/her elevated position as sufficient to ensure the effectiveness of management. He says: 'Information is the real strategy . . . if the strategists know it they behave as if they don't, their focus is on finding the right strategy not on the right information'. Information broadens a team member's vision of work and the issues with which they must grapple. Without current and relevant information, actions and decisions are likely to be based as much on assumption and prejudice as on knowledge.

To acquire the necessary information and store it can be time saving in the long term. It saves making repeated requests, and provides a basis on which to build and change to match the changing environment. By starting to store information, it is possible to develop expertise which can be left behind on departure. Many workers pay out small financial sums to families with difficulties. One team manager took the initiative and called all the 'payees' into a session with the team members. After an amusing cameo played out by the staff (to introduce the issue of repeated payments) a discussion ensued over better ways of spending the money that was relevant to the parents. They decided on a group ticket to the zoo, and other joint expenses. (Fortunately the team manager concerned saw fit to record the information on this creative initiative so that I can pass it on here! See ch 13).

The time taken to obtain relevant information will be extensive at the outset but will become less so, as only updating is required. The manager should sift information and keep a check on whether the data are useful, commensurate with the effort required to gather it.

There will be some situations which will be the reverse of this. It would be simple to argue that acquiring knowledge about the cuisine habits of private homes in terms of their adaptability to non-British meat-eating diets fulfils the needs of such a small sector as to be not worth gathering. But, where minority interests are concerned, it is important to have relevant information available to be able to respond sensitively and speedily. Fundamental respect for individual needs must underline the general guidance on 'being informed'.

Information can also show the team's own needs in relation to the wider organisation and beyond. With information, a team can make a convincing case that the action they wish to take meets the needs they defined earlier.

It seems that there is a preference for the power of statistical data, or 'number crunching'. Manipulation of hard data can be very impressive. Sometimes, though, however sophisticated the presentation, it is dry and inert — it does not seem to connect with the reality of the world.

How well do our statistical reports and analyses communicate? How lively and descriptive are they? Do they force the recipients actively to consider the implications or to accept them passively? Do they provoke further questions? Creativity and imagination are essential for effective presentation. A new angle and insight can often provide a persuasive argument for more resources. To achieve an environment where soft data alone are viewed as an adequate basis for resource allocation, managers would need to do a great deal of ground work with senior managers and politicians. Until then the use of illustrative statistics interwoven with soft data is a useful and relevant way of achieving success. A team under some pressure to justify its suboffice base at a time of budget cuts was able to engage local tenants in endorsing the benefits of the team's presence. These soft views and examples of the work achieved were mixed with hard data that showed a significant percentage reduction of mental health sections, children in care and child abuse registrations (as they were then called). The mix was irresistible and the team was not only drawn into the area base but was promoted as an example of good practice.

Information media

If information is to be useful, it has to be dynamic and mobile (communicable). Three types of information medium that can be used by the information conscious manager are grouped in Table 10.1.

Table 10.1

Face to face	Administrative	Mechanical
Information exchanges	Reframe index system	Telephone
Quality circles	Reframe referral system	Computer
Communication groups	Information systems	Newsletter
Team meetings	Mapping resources	Information services
Consultation		
Information networks		Fax
Questionnaires		Dictaphone

Face to face media

Information exchanges   These occur when people meet with the expressed purpose of giving other people information about what they are doing, or are planning to do. It can be a brief session at the beginning of a meeting, or exist in its own right. A labelled 'exchange forum' can help colleagues gain a common consciousness. It also helps avoid duplication of effort and engages fellow workers in offering their own information that is relevant to the plan or action. It is advisable to get staff to prepare in advance even with just a few notes, and to expect to spend no more than a few minutes on the exchange. Headings relevant to use would be:

We, I am (are) working on . . .
We, I am (are) working with . . .
We, I am (are) going to . . .
Did you know that . . .?

An information exchange should not inhibit spontaneity, but should ensure that information is heard by all. Information exchange shows that the manager sees the worker and consumers as potential partners in problem-solving.

Quality circles   'Promoting information exchange was the original purpose of quality circles in Japan.' Richard Chonberger (world class manufacturing) from these origins has developed a system which can be illustrated:

1. Information exchange→   2. Identification of problems→

3. Options to resolve→   4. Decision for action→

5. Evaluation→   6. Information exchange→2.

All members of quality circles are specifically trained in the process. They take responsibility for actioning decisions, they represent all levels in the organisation, and issues are initiated from below. A senior manager will participate, but will not act as chairperson. This is to avoid any mimicking of a traditional managerial meeting where hierarchical position is at the fore. Members act as equal contributors and each carries responsibility for putting into action at their level, or within their unit, the changes needed to improve quality. The intention is that quality has to be aimed for at every point within the organisation, hence every level has to participate in solving quality problems and has to be informed to do so. More agencies are raising quality as a central issue, and managers at all levels should be aware of the structure and ethos of quality circles. To be successful, the quality circle will need to have the commitment of all participants, and the organisation leaders, but without hierarchical power games coming into play.

Communication groups   These are similar to information exchanges but are likely to include staff and/or consumers from outside the agencies. The setting-up period will be lengthy as there will not be a foundation of interpersonal knowledge and experience. It will also take time to strip out jargon and check that the information being exchanged is adequately understood. Long-term benefits will be acquired for people who ensure that the extension of knowledge and understanding between people aiming to develop partnerships actually takes place. The most common format for communication groups is a lunch where staff invite local workers in to 'get to know each other'. There has to be real effort and energy put into talking with as many people as possible. (Maybe a team prize for the most information gained!) If the lunches become part of the culture of the work, then a broad attendance which adequately represents the ethnicity of the locality, as well as a gender balance, is valuable.

Team meetings   These are the most familiar form of information exchange. Most workers are likely to have participated in them. They are well placed for the formal information exchange. They can be open to special visits from others whose work may enhance the knowledge base of the team. Regular weekly or two-weekly team meetings are an excellent opportunity for ensuring that administrative staff are involved. Meetings can begin with an 'information exchange'. (Each member of the team gives a brief synopsis of his/her current work.) Administrative staff can be sources of information; they may have new ideas about organising the data; they may be able to answer queries about the organisation of the team's work. They may not have enough work to do to keep them motivated, and involving them in setting up a system for recording data or information storage may be a welcome stimulant. All this information is of considerable use to the manager, the team as a whole and, albeit indirectly, to the consumer as well. Any discussions which follow the exchange of information should be chaired in such a way that administrative staff accept that it is 'normal', in such a set-up, for them to contribute to any issues which may affect policy. Chairing and minute-taking should be rotated so that all team members have a try at a skill, new to some, in a safe environment. Access to this kind of forum is essential if the team is going to operate cohesively and efficiently.

Consultation   This is often raised when changes are afoot, when there is a need for particular information to support or reject a proposed outcome. But all too often it can be tokenistic. Staff have a responsibility to request consultation, and managers should offer it. Consultation is a gathering of soft data, usually the views of workers about a specific event or plan. The more familiar the process is, the more efficient and effective it will become. The consultation can vary from a sheet on the wall asking for comments to formal structured meetings. Even a chat on the 'phone can be more valuable than failing to ask staff their views. Without participation from the outset, any initiative will be resisted unless the implications for staff are clear. The same can be said of obtaining the views of the public, although there would have to be adjustments. Not everyone is happy to fit into the bureaucratic frameworks which may allow for organisational efficiency in information gathering. The framework for imparting or gathering information has to be consumer sensitive.

Information networks   These tend to be more informal and less easy to identify. They do not meet in a room at a time but are an organic set of relationships drawn upon for information according to their perceived knowledge and expertise. They are likely to be swung into action around problem-solving. The parts of the network drawn upon will depend upon the nature of the problem. The network exists in the mind and life of the person initiating contact with its member parts and probably would not conceive of itself as a whole entity.

What a manager needs to know about administrators

Administrative support to information management

Information can be reframed within the existing static systems. In a traditional indexing system, data are stored by name. However, this prevents an overview of the proximity of users to each other. If the system was cross referenced to include addresses, then the team might be surprised to discover, for example, that 70% of the work comes from just two roads! It would also raise issues on housing allocation, neighbourhood interactions and other poor levels of communication. It may also offer the opportunity to rationalise the allocation of staff time to particular families in the locality.

There are many more examples of how administrative information can be reframed. By making administration sympathetic to practice, the service can become more effective improving job satisfaction.

Information systems   These are usually run by administrators. Setting it up, however, may require the guidance of a library or library service information officer. It is rare, though, for administrators to be any better prepared to set up a system than the manager him/herself.

A regularly sifted, system, will ensure that information is accessible and ordered.

Questionnaires can be used to find out information from resident staff and local people. It is advisable to obtain expert advice from a researcher before undertaking the activity. The wording will need to be formulated carefully to ensure that useful data is forthcoming and that it relates to an identified purpose. The manager who finds out staff views before acting will gain more respect/popularity than the one who does not. When a number of staff are being questioned, a survey can be more manageable than trying to record free-flowing conversations. The questionnaire can be by personal interview with the manager, or between staff and consumer. This is time consuming but obtains a better response rate than a postal system which on average, only trawls a 15% response.

Mapping resources

A visual method for storing some forms of information is a map of the locality. If size permits, then a coded system of coloured pins could be used to identify referral types, and resources, both human and inert. This gives a quick presentation of the barren and bombarded areas. Those bombarded might suggest a change of approach is needed! A smaller and more flexible system can be achieved by using OHP acetates overlaid onto the reduced map. Each acetate can carry information on an aspect of the locality. When placed upon each other, a picture can be built up of the multiple dimensions of a locality.

Foci of information

An area profile This is a format which will ensure that the manager and team know what the area they work in is really about.

There is likely to be a mix of hard and soft data and to require updating to remain relevant. Developing a store of information about a community is best done by those responsible for providing the service. It may be tempting to hand over to a student, but the process of finding out means meeting people, getting personal knowledge and becoming known in the area which will be lost if the task is left to a student. It is an ideal activity for team building. Everyone can participate and take a share of the community served. As data is gathered, it can be shared at team meetings and thus help to form a common foundation for the team. How to undertake an area profile in more detail is presented in *Developing Community Social Work in teams*, Hearn and Thomson, (1987), or a more complex version is to be found in *Strategies and Tactics* (1985), Miller and Scott (NISW publications).

Internal profiles   These provide information for the purposes of human resources management which is a key task for the manager.

Training profile   This may be initiated by the training division (if one exists), who then provide a framework. The profile may require the manager and worker (or team), to sit together and clarify the training need. This will be in terms of previous experience, the skills required by the agency and future career plans. It should include the requirements laid upon an agency by new legislation and policies. Regular updating and checking that the profile is acted upon, eg that training is found, are both managerial tasks.

Career appraisal   Some agencies have requirements for regular appraisal of staff and thereby set a framework. It is essential that careers are appraised if staff are to feel valued and understand which areas they need to work on in order to keep their career moving. There are a range of informative texts on career appraisal. Current advice should be available from the personnel department.

Skills inventory   While staff may work in close proximity to one another, it must not be assumed that they have a full picture of their respective skills. Without it, they will not be able to draw on each other to provide a more effective service and a medium of mutual learning will be lost. Developing a skills inventory is best achieved by taking an initial two to three hours out of one day. The inventory should include information on personal, professional and developing skills. The list is generated by each individual, of themselves, then the rest of the team challenge and add to the lists of each other according to how they perceive their colleagues' skills. There should be no restriction on what is listed. One never knows what skills may be needed.

If kept on display, the accumulative list of skills can act as a reference and will probably boost morale. It is also a means of helping staff feel valued as whole people, which models how they should relate to their clients.

Information flows   These are as important as the information itself. The problems arise when people fail to get the information they need, or when data processing becomes difficult owing to obstacles in its passage. I was once coordinating a group. A member sent me a paper about our next meeting with a compliment slip. I read and filed this until the day. At the meeting no one else had received the paper. The originating member had expected my section to photocopy and circulate the information — but he admitted that he had not specified this! Poor communication had prevented the flow of information. It is useful to take a step back and create a diagram of the flow (Fig. 10.1), which can help place, in sharp relief, any problems which could arise.

By creating a visual pathway of how the information flows from one point to another, it is possible to identify a break in the circuit and rectify it.

It would be all too tempting as a new manager to drown oneself in data in the hope of gaining useful information. So, remember, above all, keep it simple. Ask yourself, your team and even the agency:

'Do we need this data and why?'
'Are reasons for its use still valid?'
'Can other data substitute?'
'Could it be replaced by another existing form?'
'Can we cut it out and remain efficient?'
'How often have we used it in the last year?'

Information is an essential tool but should not become an obsession.

In 1956, Marks & Spencers decided that more information was flying around the system than was useful, and was eating up their precious human resources. The company began 'Operation Simplification'. Over one year, 26 million forms were deleted from use!

References

Peters and Waterman (1982). *The Renewal Factor*. Harper and Row.
Jan Carlzon (1987). *Moments of Truth*. Ballinger.

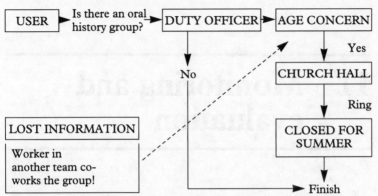

Instead of a singular linear approach, the duty officer needs to use a wider network.
Crucial information is lost by this singular approach.

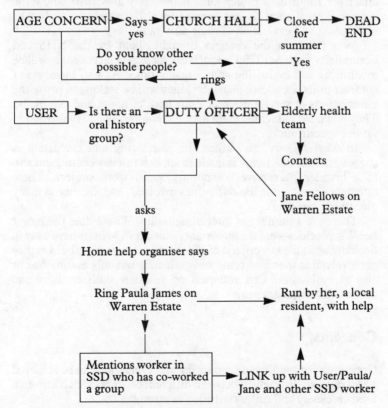

Fig. 10.1 Example of information flow

11 Monitoring and evaluation

Do we know if our services and the style we use to manage them are effective? Inquisitive professional managers will wish to know the answer even if they do not receive formal requests to undertake monitoring and evaluation of their activities.

As a result of the changes brought about by the NHS and Community Care Act 1990, social work managers increasingly will be monitoring and evaluating other organisations. As staff members of contract units, or as care managers, they will be seeking to prove the effectiveness of service delivery units both in-house and externally. They will need to include guidelines on monitoring and evaluation in service specifications.

In what follows, an outline for monitoring and evaluation is suggested, and an attempt is made to apply it to a day centre, and also to a broader preventive community social work project. These attempts demonstrate the difficulties involved, and identify as many questions as answers.

There are a number of interesting issues. Where does the power lie? Who decides what the important issues are? Do users have a say in deciding what the key criteria of effectiveness are going to be? Do they get involved in the monitoring and evaluation not only as subjects but also as evaluators? Can you pass on research skills to users and community organisations?

Concepts

Greater understanding of monitoring and evaluation can be achieved by learning to distinguish between different concepts which are often used carelessly and cause confusion as a result.

Monitoring or evaluation

Monitoring means the collection of information. Often, that is all there is to it. Evaluation follows if you apply your analytical and argumentative mind to drawing conclusions from the information.

A great deal of energy is wasted on collecting information, which, if you are lucky, gets organised into lists and charts, but is never used for reflective analysis.

Measures and methods of measurement

It will be important to distinguish between measures and methods of measurement.

Measures are criteria which you choose to define good practice. An early task will be to define these, as we will discuss. For example, a key measure might be numbers on the child protection register, but these figures, if used barely, may appear to assume that all those registered require protection, which they may not. Hence, it may be obscure as a measure of good practice and only measure levels of activity.

Methods of measurement are ways in which you acquire the information you need, and will be determined by your measures. If your measures are people's reflective personal opinions, your method might be an in-depth unstructured interview, rather than, say, a postal questionnaire. Teams sometimes make the mistake of choosing the methods of measurement before the measures. For example, they may decide to get their information by setting up group discussions among staff, but make this decision before they know what they want to find out. Later, they may realise that in order to explore the measures that become important — personal opinions held about their career progress, for example — the method should have been one-to-one interviews.

Types of measures: quantitative or qualitative?

Managers are familiar with the struggle between quantity and quality — the sheer volume of work undertaken versus its quality. Agencies can encourage emphasis on quantity by, for example, choosing, as a measure of success, the crude numbers of people using a centre (as a basis for a staffing review perhaps) rather than the intensity of their needs or quality of the rehabilitation offered. To counter this, you may wish to emphasise qualitative measures, or a combination of both.

This distinction is not between measures where you add up

numbers and those where you do not. Qualitative measures may still require you to define different categories, and check out the numbers which fit each category.

Dimensions of measures

I have found it helpful to use a list of six dimensions of measures, each of which has both quantitative and qualitative aspects. I will attempt to demonstrate this by looking at a day centre for disadvantaged elderly people.

The list of six consists of two preliminary measures (needs and resources) and four performance measures (inputs, processes, short- and long-term outcomes).

Preliminary measures (1–2)

When you are itemising what you do, you will need preliminary measures or criteria to distinguish between different kinds of need and different levels of resources. At this stage, you are not yet measuring performance, but you are establishing a language for your evaluation.

Needs addressed You may wish to reassure yourself that you are gearing your service towards the most needy users, and so classify potential users according to degree of need. It might be possible to do this quantitatively, eg those who need x and $x + 3$ hours per week of day-care service. Or you may try to do it qualitatively by establishing measures according to how many demands may be made on your most qualified or scarce staff by different users.

Resources available This requires measures which distinguish between types of resources, especially if you are going on (3–6) to compare one performance with another. You might measure resources quantitatively, eg budget available per client, or qualitatively, eg ratio of qualified to unqualified staff.

Performance measures (3–6)

These can be used to distinguish between different elements of performance.

Inputs of services You need to itemise the services available, according to measures you choose as relevant. This dimension is often neglected because so many services are taken up fully and therefore the service is recorded as an output. However, in a day centre you might have places not taken up because of transport difficulties, or an OT service neglected because old people refuse to go to the relaxation group. So, a profile of inputs would list services available, eg numbers of places available for full day/half day, services available according to degree of severity of need, eg volunteer input for minor needs, speech therapy for major handicap.

Processes and procedures The way things are done can be as important (to both staff and users) as the outcomes, and your evaluation may wish to record this. You will need to establish your measures of good processes and procedures in advance, before you begin counting them. You might, for example, place a high value on involving old people and their carers closely in regular and time-consuming reviews, and seek to record this, eg hours spent on reviews, or numbers of carers brought in for reviews. Or you may wish to stress the good team work among the staff, and seek measures to show this, for example, the numbers of people participating in a range of decisions according to complexity of decision. Of course, these data are going to be rough and ready, but it is probably important to argue for it against the grey clipboard people.

Short-term impact Short-term impact gets more attention than its bullying and neglected sibling, longer-term outcomes. The short-term impact of your centre, you might decide, is best measured quantitatively by the numbers taking up services, but you might try to measure success qualitatively, eg by asking people to identify their degree of satisfaction from a list of answers on a continuum, or by measuring take-up according to degree of need or sophistication of service received.

Preventative impact Do you ever work out how many old people you have prevented from long- or short-term residential care or hospitalisation, and estimate the likely length of that preventative impact in terms of years and months? If not, it is almost certainly because you doubt the value of your estimates, which would inevitably be quite subjective. You may also feel that this measure does not tell you enough. It might be that you succeeded in keeping people out of residential or hospital care, but were able to do little to raise their morale or improve their physical health. You might therefore prefer to use measures which discriminate between different degrees of real improvement, and count up the numbers who sustain different levels of physical or psychological improvement. This too would have a subjective element.

Choosing between measures

Unless you have a research budget almost as large as your operational budget, you will only be able to select a small number of measures. Many people opt for one or two measures of quantitative short-term impact.

Whether you go further will depend on why you are doing the evaluation as well as how much time can be spent on it.

Are you seeking further funding? If so, short-term impact data may be enough to satisfy your funder. Are you seeking to raise the morale of the team? If so, you may wish to follow users through, assessing longer-term impact. If the team is developing a culture of openness and empowerment of users, you may want to look in more detail at processes and procedures.

An equally important question is: who decides on measures? Clearly, the choosing of measures is a very powerful weapon: it involves defining what is good practice. You may wish to involve users in this process in order that the final choice of measures will reflect their views.

Taken on their own, each of these categories of measures provides only flimsy evidence of your effectiveness. How can you prove that it was *your* service (input) which caused the improvement in the old people (outcome)? You would need to have some basis for establishing a link between inputs, processes and outcomes.

To establish this link, you would need data on quantity and/or quality of inputs as well as of outputs, and also a basis for comparison. If a given level of input was followed by outcome, you might like to claim a connection. Even so, you could never be entirely sure that your input had caused the outcome; however, unless some other major factor intervened (an amazing cure for Alzheimer's Disease, a pools win shared among all the members) then the juxtaposition of the outcomes against inputs (according to the different measures chosen) would suggest that a link could be claimed. However, to be reasonably sure, you would need some basis of comparison.

The basis for comparison.

Normally, for data to reveal their meaning there has to be a baseline for comparison. It could be your last year's inputs, processes and outcomes compared with this year's, or your work this year compared to the work of the broadly similar centre 'y' down the road. Or, your work now compared against some guideline standard for day centre performance which has come out of the Department of Health amid hoots of derision. You will need to decide what basis of comparison to choose.

But, when you want to push the analysis deeper, you will find yourself delving into the preliminary measures of needs and resources. Are we dealing with greater intensity of need than last year? How has this affected performance? Are we achieving quantitative or qualitative improvements of input and/or outcome with the same, or perhaps even less staff? Or, have we got more staff but reduced our performance? If the latter, do available data give a clue as to why?

A full evaluation logically would require you to collect information under all six dimensions of measure.

Whether you can make much progress in the more sophisticated kinds of evaluation will depend on how much you can routinise and computerise the collection and organising of data. If you can use your week-by-week routine management processes to collect data on needs, resources, inputs and outcomes, which can then be crunched up by a friendly desk-top computer, you will find it easier to think in terms of evaluation. It will be much harder if you have to mount a special monitoring exercise.

Methods of measurement

By and large, research methods, like measures, fall into the two categories of quantitative and qualitative, but the distinction is not clear cut, and the methods do not correspond neatly with types of measure.

Whenever the measures involve easily verifiable facts, like numbers attending a day centre, you can use quantitative methods like a day-log. You may decide to wade through reports, files, etc (qualitative data) where you think the truth may hide, and to try to fit the stated experiences to your pre-arranged measures.

Questionnaire

Once you start to seek people's opinion, eg user satisfaction, you need more subtle methods, eg questionnaire or a semi-structured interview. Should it be a questionnaire (or schedule, in the jargon) through the post or one completed by personal interview? This will depend on resources, how accustomed to filling in questionnaires the recipients are, and how much more likely people are to tell fibs if just left with a piece of paper.

Group discussion

In seeking to identify good practice in social work settings, you may decide to rely heavily on group discussions of various kinds. You may use these to define measures, in the first place, and then to analyse performance according to these measures. Groups can be an effective way of involving staff and users in what may otherwise seem a mystifying experience.

Panel study

You bring together a sample group, eg of different categories of staff and users, with representatives from one or two other agencies. You meet periodically, say bi-monthly, to review progress. The meetings are structured, and careful recording takes place. Individual members may take on commitments for monitoring particular aspects between meetings.

Delphic study

You bring together a number of people with expert knowledge of a service. It is a shift of emphasis from a panel study, but, remember, users can be experts too. This group might meet less often than a panel once they have established the key measures for a service. They are liable to have less vested interest in the specific focus, eg when studying a particular day centre.

Tracer study

This could be carried out by a group as above or by an individual member of it; you follow a single process through all its stages.

Network analysis

You analyse who relates to whom, on what issues, over a period of time. This can reveal key factors, especially if you compare one analysis with another. It can be a particularly relevant tool if you are trying to measure the existence of 'working together' between agencies and between agencies and users.

Informant study

Someone regularly debriefs a key subject who is open to question and challenge on the content of the debrief. Developments thus are monitored by the need to prepare for the debrief. Assessment begins in preparation.

There are still a few evaluators around who turn up their noses at such so-called soft evaluation. They still feel secure with the more rigid questionnaires and 'hard facts'. However, the nature of social services work requires more subtle and penetrating methods of enquiry, even if the results are less 'scientific' and more subjective. It can be useful to think of yourself, the evaluator, as a good investigative journalist or an historian. The key is to check out both sides of any story, going out of your way to seek evidence which would contradict what most of the information seems to suggest.

Community-based practice

In a recent publication (Darvill and Smale, 1990) I collected together a number of key indicators against which to identify community-based social work. Interestingly, these serve not only as a means of identification but as measures of community-based practice.

The measures are based on the existence of:

- early warning of families at risk
- better access for people
- a negotiated response to needs
- local participation in defining services
- locally managed resources
- co-ordinated local planning

These measures derive from rather restricted kinds of 'delphic' groups, networks of community social work champions, and were not identified by users themselves as key indicators of good practice.

Early warning of families and individuals at risk

This measure could be a needs measure (we are concerned about people whose needs require a quick response), an input measure (we are available for early warnings) or a short-term impact measure (people who come to us, or are referred, are likely to come earlier). The implication is that they might present problems at an earlier stage of severity or complexity, but this needs to be proven. As an impact measure, it is qualitative.

Some teams have been able to show, with hard figures, that, compared to previous work in a centralised office, they now receive more self-referrals and that, over time, they manifest less severe problems. A consequence is that case files are closed more quickly. Fewer people are put on protection registers, or become the subjects of statutory instruments.

These measures do not define longer-term outcomes in terms of happiness or other progress. A very local office might, for example, be able to use its networks to contain people in misery and protect itself from scandal. This, of course, is unlikely, but it would be nice to prove that progress had occurred.

Better access for people

This seems to be a variant on the first measure, perhaps re-labelling the same phenomenon with less emphasis on statutory perspectives and more on the user's perspectives. It has more overtones which could make it into a process measure.

What proportion of people want their problems handled by a local office? Does the measure beg questions about users' preferences. Does it tell us anything about longer-term outcomes?

A negotiated response to needs

This is a process measure. Though useful in itself, it needs amplifying with impact or outcome measures.

Local participation in defining social services

Again, this is a process measure needing amplification.

Locally managed resources

This is a more radical kind of process measure than the last. Indeed, achievements identified by this measure may follow as the result of local participation. It might even be regarded as a short-term impact measure. But, in what ways is it in the interests of local people to manage their own services? Could their leaders get bogged down in taking over the council's worries? Could the service delivered be poor? As a measure, it has the same flaws as the last and requires to be complemented by longer-term outcome measures.

Co-ordinated local planning

This, too, is a process measure, or perhaps a short-term impact measure, and evidence would be needed of the benefit to users of co-ordinated planning. It might result in the setting up of a day centre, but is the day centre any good? And, can you link this achievement to the planning group, or might it not have happened anyhow?

Conclusion

This brief analysis is intended to show how difficult it becomes to prove the effectiveness of social service interventions. Community social work practice is certainly no woollier than traditional work in proving its long-term benefits. The criticism though is that, by and large, it has taken over a traditional approach to monitoring and evaluation, particularly as far as establishing measures is concerned.

It seems likely that the problem has come about because evaluation has established its centre of gravity in acceptable *methods* of measurement rather than measures. People have asked, for example, 'what can we show using fairly uncomplicated methods of evaluation — looking at referral statistics, analysing minutes of the community association or the team's annual work plan?'.

Much more difficult is negotiating *measures*, especially of longer-term outcomes, with a mix of people including users who will certainly between them have a wide range of views. Then you have to find ways, over a period of time, of proving that progress in these terms has occurred.

Attempts have been made to do this, eg a comparative study of two area offices in Wakefield (Hadley and McGrath, 1984) which was suitably cautious about its findings. But we must not be fazed by the traditional social work camp or by the psuedo-scientific evaluation boffins. Defining measures is a truly collective process.

References

Darvill G. and Smale, G., eds (1990). *Partners in Empowerment: Networks of Innovation in Social Work*. p 17–18, NISW.

Hadley R. and McGrath M. (1984). *When Social Services are Local*. Allen and Unwin.

Further reading

Croft S. and Beresford P. (1984). Patch and participation: the case for citizen research. *Social Work Today*, 17 September, pp 18–24.

Knapp, M. (1987). Series of seven articles starting in *Insight*, 26 June, p 13.

12 Empowerment through contracts

A core theme of this guide to new managers is empowerment. Can the social services be managed in ways which enable people who use them to discover their own power, and exercise as much control as possible over their lives?

This is the main question on which to establish a community social work critique of the NHS and Community Care Act 1990 which has sought to reorganise the social services, following the White Paper 'Caring for People'.

Clearly, feelings are mixed. Early in 1990, I attended a workshop of around 60 managers from five social services departments, and others, where the White Paper was being discussed. The managers with greatest concern for radical empowerment were in favour of the changes, even those working in SSDs dominated by a political tradition of 'we'll do it ourselves'.

Above all, the black managers welcomed the opportunities which would arise, they hoped, for ethnic minority communities to run their own services. Almost as positive were representatives from independent living schemes, self-help groups for disabled people, and people with an interest in service delivery by women's groups.

The new order will depend on central government money to ensure that standards are maintained. A great many managers will be waiting to see before they commit themselves.

My own enthusiasm for the White Paper derives from realising that the community social work needs the new legislation almost as much as the legislation needs the community social work.

Community social work managers in the 1980s were well intentioned but sometimes a little woolly — occasionally their own worst enemies. To shift ownership of social services activities towards their consumers, a firm management framework is needed, which might sharpen up community social work values and practice.

There is little new about many aspects of the 1990 NHS and Community Care Act. Social workers who have spent hours telephoning voluntary homes, hostels and family centres to find vacant places will have had much direct experience of doing deals with external agencies, for example. The agencies contracted may have received a block grant, or they may be paid from DSS funds for help to the individual. More formal contracting may involve elements of preliminary tendering (often not competitively, in the social services), a tighter definition of services and of monitoring procedures, and a legally binding agreement.

One innovation in the new era is the proposal for formal assessment and case or care management. This will identify who is entitled to received contracted services. Through one or more levels of named individuals, the assessment and care management sides will operate separately from the service provider side, and with a preset budget. This, in itself, could be used regressively, but also it has enormous potential for publicising entitlement. No wonder, some say, that care management is an area of the legislation where the Government started to drag its feet even before the ink on the White Paper was dry.

One immediate and lasting change, as a result of the legislation, will be a larger range of career options for managers, which will require careful choices to be made by those with a genuine concern for community empowerment. Should you become an assessor or care manager, or opt for service delivery, or are there other options such as contracting, inspection or handling complaints?
Let us look at each of these in turn.

Assessment and care management

During the 1980s, a number of innovations in management were incorporated into good systems of assessment, care management and care packaging.
1980s' innovations included:

- better information to the public about services available, including choices
- a stronger involvement of users and carers in negotiating packages
- the integration of other finance, eg social security payments or the user's own finance, into the resourcing of the package
- the underpinning of the agreement with a written contract

between the agency and the users

- the control by the user or family carer of the implementation of the package, or aspects of it
- the use of paid providers who merged previous roles, eg home help and auxiliary nurse roles
- the use of paid providers who come from the user's personal networks
- involvement of user's advocates in negotiating packages.

Taken together, these innovations can be used to produce a more comprehensive package of care with, and for, an individual or family and a greater sense of ownership by the user. The underpinning of assessment and care management with legislation could give considerable impetus to user empowerment.

The problem of rationing, which has always been with us (remember that telephone round), will not go away — but you cannot blame the 1990 Act for that. The key point is that managers should embrace the opportunities and make the system work their way.

Agencies will vary in whether assessment and care management is contained within one or more role and level. Assessor case managers in many agencies will be able to test the limits of their freedom. The following questions may form the basis of a checklist for someone considering a particular post.

1. Will I have the scope to extend the range of potential providers whom I shall, in effect, be funding? Will I be allowed to spend money on paying community groups and individuals to participate in packages of care? Will I be able to pay them proper working rates?

2. More importantly, perhaps, will I, or someone else, have the time to do the legwork necessary to help community groups prepare for involving themselves in service delivery? Will I be able to do development work with black and other self-help organisations? Or, does the agency think that community groups will spring into effectiveness merely by dangling opportunities in front of them?

3. Will I be able to help disadvantaged people find a voice in the assessment and care management system? This is far more than giving a seat at the assessment table to the user or the user's carer. Additionally, it will mean helping clients to understand the choices, allowing separate assessment of carers if requested, providing the option of second opinions, complaints, appeals and re-assessments as well as, ideally, developing a network of independent advocates. All this will involve time, and certainly cost money (eg payment of

advocates or at least their expenses, providing sitters to relieve carers, and so on).

4. Will I be able to introduce a staff team element into assessment and care management, without excluding those listed in 3 above?

5. Will I be able to take assessment and care management on the road, eg by having sessions in ethnically sensitive community centres where I will also have the time to make myself known and accepted?

6. Will I be able to hand over budgets to community groups or individual users, effectively delegating some aspects of assessment, most of care management as well as the service delivery system, leaving me as overall budget holder and monitor?

7. If the answer to quite a few of these is 'yes', then will I receive the training and supervision to enable me to make a go of it? Will I have the information technology I shall require?

Service delivery

Whether service delivery will be carried out mainly through in-house units of SSDs or through voluntary organisations will depend on the political colour of the local authority as well as central government financial incentives. Either way may present an opportunity for empowerment, but the manager of service delivery will have a number of options for speeding up consumer empowerment.

The checklist for a manager considering service delivery in a voluntary organisation, community or ethnic organisation may include the following:

1. Does it have a local committee which has genuine power in relation to national bodies, local funders and staff?

2. Does the organisation traditionally have self-help and campaigning roles? If so, has it sorted out where it stands on the issue of service delivery potentially driving out campaigning and self-help? Has it found ways to allow these elements to co-exist? For example, might advocacy be more effective if operating as an extension of service delivery, as some experience suggests.

3. Does it recognise the conflicting pressures on managers, given the following:
   - campaigning has to be led
   - self-help has to be nurtured
   - service delivery has to be controlled.

4. Is the committee basically competent in financial and personnel matters? If not, is it willing to learn these skills, or buy in extra help, or delegate much responsibility to managers?
5. Has the organisation contracted to allow it to employ local people? Has it negotiated reasonable job security for all staff, eg a three-year rolling budget?
6. Has it negotiated a budget which includes elements for development work and training of staff and local people?
7. Does it have effective lines of communication with potential competitors, in order to avoid destructive competition for customers or contracts?
8. Is there a good local infrastructure, eg a local council for voluntary service involved in supporting service delivery?

Contracting and other special units

Staff inside contracting or inspection units may have the greatest opportunities for radicalising the social services. The sensitive management of individual complaints may also encourage changes in mainstream services for all.

If you read over the list of questions which apply to assessors, care managers and service delivery managers, you are bound to feel that a lot depends on the framework which is imposed on the contracts. Both care managers and service delivery managers may be able to exercise some freedom to develop service delivery. These developments are likely to start from individual care managers, and there may be several care managers interfacing with one contracting unit. To ensure the continuity of innovations, a longer-term contractual frame will be needed.

A contract will need to ensure that money is available to help groups grow and develop, and, once they are operating effectively, to ensure that they receive all the help they need to cope with continuing conflicts over values and operations.

A contracting unit will also be able to exercise leadership 'from the top down', encouraging care managers to take risks. More important is setting up the community development processes which will enable local groups to truly become involved in service delivery.

Contract or inspection units will probably be in influential positions for advising local authority committees about the fundamental equity of the overall system. Are ethnic minorities, carers, disabled people and their organisations getting a fair allocation of resources?

Three-way partnership: an example

A local day centre for people recovering from mental illness, including people either discharged from psychiatric hospital, or at serious risk of admission, was run by a small local voluntary committee.

This day centre was failing in a number of respects.

- Its committee had become burnt out, and failed to exercise adequate supervision and other staff development procedures in respect of an equally burnt-out manager.
- Meaningful involvement of users, ex-users and carers in management had run into the ground.
- It was competing for referrals with an NHS day hospital which had better links with the psychiatric hospital: no one stepped in to umpire the games which were going on.
- Social workers and community nurses (including CPNs) were failing to make referrals to either unit, based on lack of knowledge and in some cases prejudice against the voluntary sector: no system existed to sort that out.

The introduction of the 1990 Act hopefully should help to reduce the incidence of this kind of problem. This will be through the statutory manager's exercise of leadership and the establishment of partnership between local authority and even the smallest local group providing a service.

Action by the care manager

Care management will make it easier to pinpoint those responsible for ensuring that referrals are made on a fair basis. Managers will also be able to monitor the service delivery to step in (or get others to) before committees and staff of services become burnt out, ie they will have a short-term role, anticipating involvement from more distant contracting and even inspection units.

Care managers, sensitive to issues of user and carer involvement, will be able to help local agencies to manage this aspect of their work: being a voluntary organisation does not, in itself, guarantee a high level of participation.

Action by the contract units

Managers of contracting units hopefully will be able to negotiate longer-term block contracts which both anticipate problems and sort them out quickly. The initial contract could stipulate the requirements for the committee in terms of supervision of the manager and user involvement. It could help the organisation sort out the balance of activities between service delivery, campaigning and self-help. In some cases, it might encourage an independent organisation to pull out of service delivery.

Action by service delivery managers

The service delivery organisation, should seek to negotiate salary and staffing levels which ensure competent managers and staff. Budgets should allow for expenses, and other incentives, to keep committees, including user representatives, motivated and fresh. Budgets should also allow for training and consultancy.

There will be problems, but the pre-1990 system when SSDs sought to do much more themselves, did not prevent situations like the example given here.

Teamwork

Effective management of a scenario such as the one given above requires a crucial area of teamwork at first-line and middle-management level. Assessors, care managers, service delivery managers (perhaps from the voluntary sector) and contract managers need to work together.

Teamwork will be essential if it is going to be possible to recognise and achieve good management practice which has been emphasised in this guide. Good management requires:

- space and time to allow the unique cultures of service delivery organisations to emerge, including black and women's cultures
- measured and reasonable risk-taking
- recognition of 'management by muddling through' as a fact of life in many situations and which can often become a strength
- the avoidance of unnecessary and destructive competition and even conflict, eg over winning contracts and contract compliance.

Community social work practice has a great deal to offer all three aspects of management in the new era. It is surely not too naive to predict the arrival of a new generation of community social work managers who are no longer marginalised in suboffices but with real opportunities to empower communities.

Further reading

A sample of the many recent articles and papers:

Ahmad, Arshi (1989). Contracts for black clients. *NCVO Community Care Newsletter*, Nov., p. 22.

Association of Metropolitan Authorities (AMA). Contracts for Social Care: the local authority view. AMA 1990.

Brandon, D. and Towe, N. Free to choose: An introduction to service brokerage. *Good Impressions* (50 Lombard Road, London SW11).

Darvill, G. (1990). *The future of domiciliary care. Report of a workshop*. Social Services Inspectorate (East Midlands).

Department of Health (SSI). Purchase of Service: Practice Guidance and Practice Material for SSDs and other Agencies. HMSO 1991.

King, J. A. (1990). Helping hand. *Community Care*, 22 Feb.

Miller, C. (1990). Continuity and change. *Insight*, 14 Mar., p. 23.

Peck, E. and Barker, I. (1990). Snakes and ladders, *Insight*, 3 May, p. 20.

Price Waterhouse/Department of Health. Implementing Community Care: Purchaser, Commissioner and Provider Roles. HMSO 1991.

Warner, N. (1990). Kent hops to it. *Insight*, 31 Jan., p. 22.

13 A manager in action: imaginative uses of Section I money

Whilst the legal section may have been renumbered under the Children Act, the action taken by Joyce and her team is very much in the spirit of partnership and innovation required of the new manager today.

In this paper, Joyce a then first-line manager shows how managers and their teams need awareness of national trends, local information and a willingness to be self-critical. It provides a real life story of a thinking and creative manager in action.

How and when social workers spend money, either directly or to provide services for families, is not just a matter of the budgets at our disposal. It involves the values we bring to our work, the assumptions we make about the causes of family breakdown, and our attitudes to parents.

The original focus of the 'Imaginative Uses of Section 1 Money' workshop was some preventative work undertaken by a team of social workers in an inner city social services. A discussion about assumptions formed the first part of the workshop. In the second part, participants were asked to develop a theory of 'normalisation' for working with families. Research does not help very much in telling us which methods of prevention are successful. Trying to develop a range of services which 'normal' families use, as a matter of course, when bringing up children is perhaps as good a starting point as any. The work of the social work team forms the third section.

The work of Holman (1985), Packman (1986) and Jordan (1982)

as well as my own research has been influential in developing my ideas in describing and analysing the workshop.

Assumptions

1. There is a strong link between poverty and social deprivation and reception or committal to care.

The link shows up when the social factors associated with children in care are defined.

- *Single parents* Of children in care, 60 % come from families with a single parent. The Finer Committee reference pointed out that single parents are the section of the population most likely to be poor.
- *Large families* Whereas 3% of families have five children or more, 18% of applications for reception into care come from such families. Of large families, 69 % live at, or below, the poverty line.
- *Unskilled manual workers* Of the population, 10% according to the Registrar General are in this class while 45% of children in care come from the lowest social class.
- *Low income* Of families with children in care, 75 % were below the official poverty line and more than 50 % were on state benefits.
- *Inadequate housing* Various studies record that children in care tend to come from overcrowded homes or homes lacking basic amenities. (Figures from Holman, 1985.)

Put together, the evidence suggests that poor children are more likely to come into care, and indicates that the reasons for reception into care cannot be attributed wholly to family interaction.

2. Poverty has an effect on behaviour and family functioning. Poverty, for instance, contributes to:

- ill health which can impair parenting capacities
- the lack of resources, such as toys, for socialising children
- parents being deprived of self-respect and self-esteem, which can lead to depression or aggression
- the inability of the wider family network to offer help to children when there is a problem within the immediate family.

The presenting behaviour problems of depression or neglect are highlighted, while all too often the deprivation is ignored.

3. The use of social services resources, including Section 1 money, will not alter the structural inequalities of poor housing and poverty, but this is no reason for ignoring the consequences of them, or for not using our resources to help alleviate them.
4. Although, as a profession, we would say that preventing children coming into care was the main task, the results of our professional deliberations and negotiations with governments and elected members seem to deny this.

- A major piece of legislation, the 1975 Act, made no mention of prevention: instead, it concentrated on making it easier to sever links between parents and their children.
- The differences between local authority budgets for dealing with children in care, and those trying to prevent care, are enormous. In my own authority, the boarding-out budget is £1.9 million, heading for a £220 000 overspend, while the Section 1 budget £60 000. This is not unusual. Across the country, Section 1 budgets tend to be underspent.
- Look at the specialist child-care workers in your department. There are many with titles such as senior caseworker (fostering and adoption) but few senior caseworkers (prevention).
- Day-care places have been reduced from 65 000 just after the war to 25 000 in 1984. Many of these places are now being turned into family centres which do not offer resources to a single parent wanting to work or even wanting a break from the children. Studies have shown a correlation between the provision of day care and a reduction in admission to care (reported in Holman, 1985). Extension of day-care provision was one of the main recommendations of the Finer Committee.

The House of Commons select committee commented that 'if as much money and intellectual thought went into prevention as it does into securing substitute homes for children, we might be on the way to formulating a preventative strategy and a service of family support'.

5. As a profession, we are split between two major value systems which influence the way in which individual workers and departments perceive family breakdown and attempt to prevent it.
   The split is illustrated in, for example, the two minority reports that came out of the Barclay Committee and an article in the *British Journal of Social Work* (1982) by Lorraine Fox. The

differences are complex. If you ask a group of social workers what prevention means, the answers are likely to range:

- from giving money — to giving therapy
- from the offer of a volunteer — to the offer of a senior practitioner
- from a childminder — to a parenting skills course
- from maintaining the family unit — to rescuing the children.

The main Barclay Report and the BASW Code of Practice on Prevention and Rehabilitation try to synthesise the two value positions and let's hope that future research can point us in one direction.

Towards a theory of 'normalisation'

In the meantime, we do have resources at our disposal, and we need to make decisions as to how to use them.

Normalisation is now an accepted theoretical base for working with people with a mental or physical handicap. It may be of use in developing a strategy of prevention.

The workshop participants were asked the question 'What resources do we, or our friends, call upon to ease the burden of bringing up children?'

Forty five items were listed. They can be summarised as:

- a regular partner to share the care
- grandparents or friends who are willing and able to take the children for a weekend or at a time of crisis
- membership of a babysitting circle
- not necessarily a lot of money but some put by for an emergency, such as the washing machine breaking down.
- the intellectual and/or financial ability to entertain children
- the energy and organisational skills for parents to do something for themselves — whether it's a nightclass or a regular night out
- emotional health and support
- good housing, transport and shops
- an occasional holiday
- some domestic help.

If these normal resources are lacking, because you are a lone parent or on supplementary benefit, or because you are not on speaking terms with your family, or because you are unable to sustain friendships and relationships, then looking after your children will be difficult.

If we believe that it is our job to prevent children coming into care, then we need to, at least, ensure that all parents have the resources which ordinary families have to do their job of parenting. It would seem premature to talk about inadequate parenting before those parents have had a chance to show that they value the same things for their children, and for themselves, as we do.

Another question was then posed in the workshop. 'What could we provide, or ensure is available in the community, to make up for the lack of privately available resources?' Twenty two 'services' were listed, including:

- babysitting services
- domiciliary help
- welfare rights advice to maximise income; credit unions
- foster parents, or rent-a-granny, for speedily self-organised respite care
- toys and equipment at home
- play facilities outside the home
- volunteers to befriend children
- day care for under 5s, and holiday and after-school care for school-age children
- social activities for parents
- money when a crisis occurs
- advocacy over housing and planning issues.

One final question was asked. 'Who should be provided with these preventative resources?' A concept of normalisation would suggest that provision should be as extensive as possible — a social service rather than a residual service. Evidence to support this comes from the fact that children on 'at risk' registers are less likely to come into care than other children known to social service departments, presumably because social work resources are concentrated on this minority group. We seem to be missing those families whose children do end up in care.

Working with money

The work that a team of social workers in an inner city authority undertook was neither extremely imaginative or unusual. But it does demonstrate ways of working, within the constraints of child care legislation, with families who are poor and who see their problems as financial.

The various projects came about from intense dissatisfaction with the way we were working with a group of families who were continually asking for Section 1 money.

From discussions in team meetings, it became apparent that as a group of workers, we were feeling used, abused and conned. We were feeling angry with the clients and were becoming punitive and judgemental. We were also beginning to talk about 'solving the problem' by just saying 'No.'

We drew back and on reflection decided that we were blaming the clients for being poor, and not accepting that lack of money was a real social work problem.

Once we had accepted this, it allowed us to believe that it was legitimate for us to work positively with money problems rather than grudgingly.

Over the next few months, we developed a strategy which, while not altering the structural causes of poverty, allowed the clients a chance to define their own needs, and helped us to service the demands made upon us.

The first step was to call a meeting of the parents who were being given regular amounts of money. Not surprisingly, the 16 names were all young single mothers, all on supplementary benefit; about half had allocated social workers; nearly all had day-care places and five had had their children in care.

We wrote to them explaining that we wanted to talk to them about our unhelpful and unfair reactions when they came in asking for money.

Our aims for the meeting were:

- to ask for their ideas as to how we could help with money problems
- to discuss three ideas we had
- to give them knowledge of the framework and constraints we worked under

Although only seven people turned up, we knew the bush telegraph would work effectively.

Three workers organised the meeting, and we began with a role play of what happened behind the scenes when they came to ask for money. Amongst much laughter as they tried to guess which one of them the social worker was role playing, and amongst much indignation as they heard our cynical responses to their needs, I think we achieved some understanding. When they read the words of Section 1 of the Act, and saw the forms we had to fill in, they were shocked at the emphasis on reception into care and on the amount of form filling 'just for two quid'. They also told us of some of the ways they conned us!

We then told them our ideas which were accepted with understandable scepticism and were eventually put into practice:

1. *A set rate of payment*   If we agreed that they were entitled to money for subsistence, we would use a set rate based on Department of Health and Social Security (now DSS) urgent needs payment rates. This, as we had hoped, reduced the power battles between worker and client as the latter pleaded and the former made a 'judgement'. It also made us realise that we had probably increased their stress with the low amounts of money we had given them previously.

2. *An urgent needs payment project*   By training a group of workers and volunteers in the complexities of urgent payment regulations, and being available each day for a month to accompany clients to the DSS, we hoped to pass on some negotiating and advocacy skills, clarify their rights as regards DSS and increase their, and our, self-esteem by focusing energy at the DSS rather than at each other. For a short while the project succeeded in getting the DSS to pay out. It also reduced our Section I spending!

3. *A budgeting group*   We suggested a group who would focus on money matters and on how they could maximise their income. We allowed £100 Section 1 money for the group to spend as they wished. The group definitely taught the social workers more than the clients about the art of living on a low income. Sadly, and surprisingly, most of the £100 was returned unspent. The group developed into a self-determining activity-based group where much-needed friendships began.

We ended the meeting with their ideas on how we could use Section 1 money to help them most. They had no problems at all explaining to us — very movingly — what the pressures were when you lived month in and month out on such a low income. 'No treats and no clothes for the children or for themselves.'

They gave us a graphic picture of bored children, guilty mothers; demanding children, desperate mothers. To deprive their children of the treats which other children had, made them feel bad mothers. With few family or personal resources to call upon, they did the obvious thing. They would spend their DSS money on the children or on themselves. Debts would pile up bringing further stress and anger. Coming to the social services was their last resort.

What could we do? Buy a family zoo ticket that we can borrow, suggested one; set up a clothing store, said another.

And so we did. With money in hand and negotiations with the zoo, the 'parents group' had their name on two tickets which allowed free entry to the zoo. A booking system through the receptionist and duty social worker allowed them to plan their 'treats' for holidays and weekends. On the rare occasions that the tickets were not returned, one of the parents would go and sort it out!

The clothing store — not a swap shop, they insisted, as they had nothing to swap — never worked quite as well. We invested £100 Section 1 money in rails, an iron and storage. We negotiated space in a local community hall and found volunteers to run it. There were difficulties in keeping it going, but it always revived.

All so simple, so obvious, so normal and so cheap. Why had we not thought of their ideas before? Because, I suspect, poverty still makes social workers feel uncomfortable. Money problems are referred on to the DSS or to the Citizens Advice Bureau. Those real feelings of being bad mothers caused by poverty are seen by social workers as relationships problems between parents and children. When normal, ordinary resources are needed — resources that any family would expect when bringing up their children — we only offer them lessons in parenting skills.

By listening to what they had to say, and seeing them first as they saw themselves — people with money problems — we were able to shift the relationship between worker and client some way towards honesty and respect.

References

Fox, L. (1982). Two value positions in recent child care law and practice. *British Journal of Social Work*.

Holman, R. (1985). Inequality in child care. *Family Rights Group*.

Jordan, B. (1986). Is prevention a rude word? Paper given at the NCB organised Conference October.

Packman, J. Randall, J. and Jacques, N. (1986) *Who needs Care*, Blackwell.

DHSS (1974), Sir Morris Finer. Report of the Committee on One Parent Families